Key Topics in Attitudes and Persuasion

This book offers an accessible introduction to psychological theories of attitudes, attitude change, and persuasion. It explores questions of what attitudes are, how people form different attitudes, and how these attitudes can be changed.

This book guides readers through five core sections that examine the essential properties and components of attitudes, key theoretical frameworks explaining attitude formation and change, methodologies for measuring and assessing attitudes, real-world applications across diverse domains, and cutting-edge research and emerging trends. It looks at how attitude theory can be applied to health behaviours, political decision-making, marketing strategies, and environmental sustainability initiatives. This book also presents valuable insights into recognising and defending against manipulative persuasion techniques, from propaganda to deception in the marketplace.

By highlighting the profound influence attitudes exert on human behaviour, this book serves as essential reading for students of social psychology, applied psychology, sociology, political science, communication, marketing, and management. It will also be of interest to anyone interested in knowing more about the psychology behind persuasion and attitudes.

Wojciech Cwalina is Professor and Head of the Department of Social Psychology at the Maria Curie-Skłodowska University in Lublin, Poland.

Paweł Koniak is an Assistant Professor at the Department of Social Psychology, Maria Curie-Skłodowska University, Lublin, Poland.

BPS Key Topics in Psychology

British Psychological Society

Routledge, in partnership with the British Psychological Society (BPS), is pleased to present *BPS Key Topics in Psychology*, a series of short introductory books that focus on a specific field within psychology. Each book is broken down into bitesize chunks to provide a helpful overview of core psychology topics, made clear by a five-part structure: foundations, theories, methodologies, impacts, and emerging areas. Written by active and experienced authors, these essential books encourage students to approach fundamental concepts with confidence and critical thinking.

Books may incorporate student-friendly pedagogies, including tools such as feature boxes, key terms and definitions; and links to further reading online. Concise yet comprehensive, these books offer a simple and accessible overview of core psychology topics for students looking for a summary of key concepts in the topic, or those new to the area.

Key Topics in Coaching Psychology
Rebecca J. Jones and Holly Andrews

Key Topics in Educational Psychology
Lisa Marks Woolfson

Key Topics in Forensic Psychology
Terri Cole and Dara Mojtahedi

Key Topics in Children's Emotional Development
Dale Hay

Key Topics in Attitudes and Persuasion
Wojciech Cwalina and Paweł Koniak

For more information about this series, please visit: www.routledge.com/BPS-Key-Topics-in-Psychology/book-series/BPSKTP

Key Topics in Attitudes and Persuasion

Wojciech Cwalina
and Paweł Koniak

LONDON AND NEW YORK

Designed cover image: Getty Images

First published 2026
by Routledge
4 Park Square, Milton Park, Abingdon, Oxon OX14 4RN

and by Routledge
605 Third Avenue, New York, NY 10158

Routledge is an imprint of the Taylor & Francis Group, an informa business

British Library Cataloguing-in-Publication Data
A catalogue record for this book is available from the British Library

ISBN: 9781032963471 (hbk)
ISBN: 9781032963464 (pbk)
ISBN: 9781003589174 (ebk)

DOI: 10.4324/9781003589174

Typeset in Galliard
by codeMantra

Access the Support Material: www.routledge.com/9781032963464

Contents

Foreword

In the modern world, problems constantly arise that require solutions at the level of individuals, groups, countries, and international organisations. Persistent prejudices against minorities (ethnic or sexual), wars and related propaganda, climate change, and political populism are areas where knowledge about attitudes and their shaping is essential. Understanding the importance of attitudes in driving human behaviour and how they can be changed seems to be an obvious starting point for initiatives aimed at increasing the well-being of individuals.

Attitudes, how people evaluate various objects around them, are force shaping what governments do (as government need to align with people's preferences), who is in government (as it is a consequence of citizens' attitudes toward politicians and parties), what consumers buy, how patients behave, what people do in their everyday life, what citizens support, and what they oppose.

It is no wonder that many forces in the world wish to shape the attitudes of the people. Some of these persuaders are friendly and want to convince people for what is good, while others are not, and want to manipulate, deceive, and convince people to evaluate good things negatively and bad things positively.

The aim of this book is to provide an accessible introduction to psychological theories of attitudes and their change. The main reason for undertaking theoretical analyses and research on attitudes is the belief that this construct would explain people's preferences to treat entities with favour or disfavour. In other words, attitude is considered a construct that helps explain human behaviour in relation to various objects (e.g., other people, social groups, or political issues) from the simplest and most ordinary acts to the highly complex and rare ones.

In this book, we concisely show what attitudes are, their properties and functions, how they are formed, and how they can be changed. We also present main theories of attitudes and persuasion, with their consequences for changing attitudes in advertising, health domain, politics, intergroup relations, and environmental issues. We also show the emerging areas of attitude and persuasion studies: how the practice of attitude change appears in times of tailored messages, a globalised world, and the reality of echo chambers. We also demonstrate how to defend against malevolent persuasion, deception in the marketplace, and propaganda.

The concept of attitudes has been present in psychology since the beginning of the 20th century. Since then, there has been a significant increase in psychological knowledge, and social psychology has emerged as a separate field.

It is therefore not surprising that the topic of attitudes is an integral part of every social psychology textbook. However, there are usually single chapters devoted to attitudes, which are relatively general. However, published books devoted solely to attitudes are aimed primarily at scientists, and their language may not be accessible to undergraduate students. Furthermore, the content in these books covers very specific issues within the theory of attitudes and attitude change.

In this context, we believe that a book on attitudes addressed to students of various knowledge disciplines may be an important filler of the gap, enabling the acquisition of basics, but not general knowledge about attitudes, their relationship with behaviour and persuasion processes.

We would also like to thank all those who made this book possible. To the British Psychological Society for a new series of short books focusing on a specific field within psychology, in which our book on attitudes and attitude change is published. We especially thank our editor at Routledge, Emilie Coin. Her patience, understanding, and encouragement, as well as her attention to technical details, were invaluable. We also thank the anonymous reviewers, whose comments significantly influenced the content presented in this book.

We are especially grateful to our families. No one knows better than our wives and daughters how daily lives change when husbands and fathers decide to write a book.

Part 1

Key Foundations

This section in summary

- The definition of attitude and its structure
- The basic functions of attitudes
- The genetic and learning-based sources of attitudes
- The impact of attitudes on attention, memory, and information processing
- The influence of attitudes on behaviour
- The persuasion and attitude change
- The variables in persuasion: source, message, channel, receiver, context, and object
- The cognitive dissonance theory

DOI: 10.4324/9781003589174-1

Chapter 1

Defining Attitudes

The concept of attitude was established as one of the prime substantive areas of social psychology at the beginning of the 20th century in the seminal work of Thomas and Znaniecki (1918) documenting the experiences of Polish immigrants in Europe and North America. During the first third of this century, however, the study of attitudes was pursued in many disparate fields with little communication or agreement regarding its properties and boundaries. A major integrative influence was provided by Allport (1935) which brought together the divergent prior usages of attitude, distinguished it from other psychological concepts, and unquestionably established its study as a speciality of social psychology, which found full expression in his famous statement: "[The attitude] concept is probably the most distinctive and indispensable concept in contemporary American social psychology" (p. 798).

The main reason for undertaking theoretical analyses and research on attitudes was the belief that this construct would explain (to a greater or lesser extent) people's preferences to treat entities with favour or disfavour. In other words, attitude is considered a construct that helps explain human behaviour in relation to various objects (e.g., other people, social groups, or political issues) from the simplest and most ordinary acts to the highly complex and rare ones.

However, early research results have already begun to show that the attitude-behaviour relationship is weak and that the predictive power of attitudes is relatively limited. As a result, some researchers began to question the meaning of using this construct in psychology. The apogee of this movement was the work of Wicker (1969), who analysed 42 studies in which correlations between attitude and behaviour were very weak and insignificant.

Dominant attempts to solve this problem have focused on the development of attitude theory and more precise measurement methods (see e.g., Banaji & Heiphetz, 2010; Ostrom, 1968). It can be argued that the modern understanding of attitudes and the multitude of studies demonstrate that the second approach was successful. Nevertheless, throughout

DOI: 10.4324/9781003589174-2

all these years of research and theoretical analysis, the fundamental question has been, and remains, "What is an attitude?"

Attitude. A psychological tendency expressed by evaluating a particular entity (or object) with some degree of favour or disfavour.

One of the first answers to the question "What is an **attitude**?" was provided by Allport (1935, p. 810): "An attitude is a mental and neural state of readiness, organized through experience, exerting a directive or dynamic influence upon the individual's response to all objects and situations with which it is related." This understanding of attitude is relatively general and emphasises the aspect linking it to the individual's behaviour, or more precisely, to their readiness to respond to people or events in their environment.

The relationship between attitude and behaviour was a characteristic element of almost all early approaches to attitude. From a learning theory perspective, Doob (1947, p. 136) defined it as "an implicit, drive-producing response considered socially significant in the individual's society." According to him, this response occurs within the individual (consciously or unconsciously) and is elicited by specific stimuli. Which stimuli will elicit it is the result of prior learning to generalise and discriminate between stimuli associated with rewards and punishments, that is, conditioning. Moreover, an attitude is anticipatory and mediating in nature, meaning that it precedes an overt response (e.g., a verbal statement) that is intended to bring a reward. An attitude is also drive-producing. This means that, when it is activated, tension builds within the individual, which is reduced by performing a specific behaviour.

The attitude-behaviour relationship is also emphasised in cognitive consistency theories. According to Abelson (1972, p. 28), an attitude is "a disposition to place oneself into appreciated episodes of interaction with a class of objects." It functions as a specific response programme that is "switched on" in a given situation.

In subsequent years, however, psychologists recognised that the attitude-behaviour relationship is rather an empirical issue and should not be included in the definition of attitude. The essence of an attitude is that an individual evaluates "some symbol or object or aspect of his world in a favorable or unfavorable manner" (Katz, 1960, p. 168). It is therefore a learned disposition of a person to react to a given object or class (or category) of objects positively or negatively (Katz, 1960; Osgood et al., 1957; Sherif, 1960).

Sarnoff's (1960) attempt to introduce attitudes into psychoanalytic theory also rests on the concept of attitude as an evaluative disposition to respond to a class of objects. However, according to him, "an individual's attitude towards a class of objects is determined by the particular role those objects have come to play in facilitating responses that reduce the tension of particular motives and which resolve particular conflicts among motives" (Sarnoff, 1960, p. 261). An attitude is therefore a way in which a person has learned to reduce the tension aroused by a motive (conscious or unconscious). Moreover, the attitude towards an object may or may not be consistent with the motive. When such consistency exists, the attitude anticipates those overt responses that will directly and effectively reduce the tension. Alternatively, when there is a lack of congruence, the attitude will underlie covert ego-defensive responses (e.g., projection, repression, identification with the aggressor, rationalisation, or denial), the purpose of which is, in fact, to obscure the existence of such motives. Thus, in this psychoanalytic approach, an attitude may evoke positive responses when, in reality, the object in question is "neutral" as a means of reducing tension.

It is now generally accepted that an attitude is "a psychological tendency expressed by evaluating a particular entity with some degree of favor or disfavor" (Eagly & Chaiken, 1993, p. 1). This entity is any conceivable object, including physical things, people, and groups but also issues (e.g., abortion) or abstract ideas (e.g., democracy). Most psychologists agree with the core of this definition but specific models of attitudes are much more diverse; one of the main points of discussion in this regard is how attitudes are represented or stored in an individual's memory. For example, Fazio (1986) posits that attitudes are stored as more or less strong associations between a given object and an evaluation of that object. Wilson and Hodges (1992), in contrast, argue that attitudes are formed when we need them (e.g., when someone asks about them) and are not based on attitude-object associations stored in memory but on our feelings or beliefs that are salient at a given moment. A more detailed description of these approaches can be found in the description of the structure of attitudes (Chapter 2) and theories of attitudes (Chapter 6). However, in both perspectives, the essence of an attitude is to understand it as an evaluative response to an object. Just because the evaluative dimension (positive–negative, favourable–unfavourable, good–bad) is a key aspect of attitudes does not mean that attitudes are identical with affect or emotions. Even the earliest analyses of attitudes emphasised that, in addition to the affective dimension, attitudes also have a cognitive component – beliefs about the object, its attributes, and its relationships with other objects (e.g., Katz, 1960).

The consequence of these analyses is the **tripartite model of attitudes**, also known as the ABC model, developed by Rosenberg and Hovland (1960). In this model an attitude is thought to consist of three components: affective, behavioural (conative), and cognitive. The affective component refers to (positive or negative) feelings and emotions elicited by the attitude object. The behavioural component relates to past behaviours and future intentions towards the object. In other words, these are the action tendencies of individuals to approach or avoid an object or perform some response. The cognitive component encompasses beliefs, thoughts, and evaluations about the attitude object. Research on the full tripartite model has shown that these three attitude components are distinguishable from each other but only under certain conditions (Bagozzi, 1978). For example, Ostrom (1969), examining attitudes towards the church, found that despite the consistency in responses across these components, each of them exhibited unique variance not shared by the other two. However, Kothandapani (1971), in a study of attitudes towards birth control, found that the individual components were not found to contain unique variance. These contradictory results, according to Bagozzi (1978), may be related to attitude objects or domains. Objects with which participants have extensive past experience (e.g., the church) are likely to be associated with very high intercomponent correlations. In contrast, more abstract attitude domains or those with which people have less personal experience may produce low intercomponent consistency.

The tripartite model of attitudes. In this model an attitude is thought to consist of three components: affective, behavioural (conative), and cognitive.

Affect-based attitudes. Attitudes in which the overall evaluation of an object falls closest to affect.

Cognition-based attitudes. Attitudes in which the overall evaluation falls closest to cognition.

While acknowledging these early contributions, contemporary researchers modified the tripartite model to view affect, beliefs, and behaviour as related to attitudes rather than as components of attitudes (e.g., Zanna & Rempel, 1988). In other words, an attitude can be based on three distinct classes of information: cognitive, affective, and behavioural. At first glance, this shift in approach may seem insignificant. However, this is not the case. Viewing an attitude as based on three types of information rather than as consisting of three components implies that an attitude may be based more (or exclusively) on each of these sources or on various combinations of them. Most research attention has focused on the differences between **affect-based** and **cognition-based attitudes** (e.g., Breckler & Wiggins, 1989; Crites et al., 1994). According to Chaiken et al. (1995), affectively based attitudes are characterised by the fact that the overall evaluation of an object falls closest to affect, whereas in cognitively based attitudes, the overall evaluation falls closest to cognition. Haddock and Zanna's (1998) study demonstrated that in the case of attitudes towards capital punishment, individuals with attitudes based primarily on affect relied more on their feelings in their judgements. Conversely, individuals with attitudes based primarily on cognitions relied more on their beliefs and thoughts related to this issue. Furthermore, Verplanken et al. (1998) found that affect-based evaluations are more accessible than cognition-based evaluations when the attitude object appears in our environment. Furthermore, Stangor et al. (1991) showed that affective responses to target groups are a more consistent and stronger predictor of prejudices than the content of social stereotypes. However, as emphasised by Eagly et al. (1994, p. 134),

> even if an attitude were formed by purely affective mechanisms or purely cognitive ones, it is unlikely that it would remain purely affective or purely cognitive for long, because of the synergistic relation that exists between these classes of attitudinal responses. Thus, people's affectively based attitudes would no doubt influence their subsequent cognitions, as they reflected on their feeling states. Conversely, people's cognitive appraisals of attitude objects are likely to influence their subsequent affective reactions to them.

The distinction between affect- and cognition-based attitudes also has important implications for the way in which such attitudes can be changed, whether through affective information or rather through strong arguments (see Section 12.1.3).

Early attitude theorists emphasised that we may be aware of our attitudes, but in many cases we are not even aware that we have them and that they influence our judgements and behaviours. If so, they can also be activated by a given object without the mediation of cognitions: automatically, without awareness, without intention, and efficiently in terms of the use of cognitive resources (Bargh, 1994). This observation and the results of numerous studies have shown that we can have **implicit** and **explicit attitudes** towards the same object. Greenwald and Banaji (1995) define implicit attitudes as the introspectively unidentified

> **Implicit attitudes**. The introspectively unidentified (or inaccurately identified) traces of past experience that can influence responses regarding the object, even when these experiences are not remembered or consciously accessible.
>
> **Explicit attitudes**. Conscious, deliberate, and self-reported evaluations, or beliefs that individuals hold about an object, person, or event.

(or inaccurately identified) traces of past experience that can influence responses regarding the object, even when these experiences are not remembered or consciously accessible. Implicit attitudes may be consistent with explicit attitudes, but, as is often found, they may be divergent and weakly correlated (Hofmann et al., 2005). For example, some people report no prejudice against minority groups (e.g., LGBT+), but measures of their implicit attitudes suggest that these prejudices are strong at the implicit level. Which of these attitudes, implicit or explicit, exerts a dominant influence on our judgements and behaviours, and under what circumstances, is the essence of the dual-process and dual-system models of attitudes, which are presented in Chapter 6.

Further Reading

Banaji, M. R., & Heiphetz, L. (2010). Attitudes. In S. T. Fiske, D. T. Gilbert, & G. Lindzey (Eds.), *Handbook of social psychology* (Vol. 1, 5th ed., pp. 353–393). Hoboken, NJ: John Wiley & Sons.

References

Abelson, R. P. (1972). Are attitudes necessary? In B. T. King, & E. McGinnies (Eds.), *Attitudes, conflicts, and social change* (pp. 19–32). New York: Academic Press.

Allport, G. W. (1935). Attitudes. In C. Murchison (Ed.), *Handbook of social psychology* (pp. 798–844). Worcester, MA: Clark University Press.

Bagozzi, R. P. (1978). The construct validity of the affective, behavioral, and cognitive components of attitude by analysis of covariance structures. *Multivariate Behavioral Research*, *13*(1), 9–31.

Banaji, M. R., & Heiphetz, L. (2010). Attitudes. In S. T. Fiske, D. T. Gilbert, & G. Lindzey (Eds.), *Handbook of social psychology* (Vol. 1, 5th ed., pp. 353–393). Hoboken, NJ: John Wiley & Sons.

Bargh, J. A. (1994). The four horsemen of automaticity: Awareness, intention, efficiency, and control in social cognition. In R. S. Wyer, & T. K. Srull (Eds.), *Handbook of social cognition* (pp. 1–40). Hillsdale, NJ: Lawrence Erlbaum Associates.

Breckler, S. J., & Wiggins, E. C. (1989). Affect versus evaluation in the structure of attitudes. *Journal of Experimental Social Psychology*, *25*(3), 253–271.

Chaiken, S., Pomerantz, E. M., & Giner-Sorolla, R. (1995). Structural consistency and attitude strength. In R. E. Petty, & J. A. Krosnick (Eds.), *Attitude strength: Antecedents and consequences* (pp. 387–412). Hillsdale, NJ: Lawrence Erlbaum Associates.

Crites, S. L., Fabrigar, L. R., & Petty, R. E. (1994). Measuring the affective and cognitive properties of attitudes: Conceptual and methodological issues. *Personality and Social Psychology Bulletin*, *20*(6), 619–634.

Doob, L. W. (1947). The behavior of attitudes. *Psychological Review*, *54*(3), 135–156.

Eagly, A. H., & Chaiken, S. (1993). *The psychology of attitudes*. Fort Worth, TX: Harcourt Brace Jovanovich College Publishers.

Eagly, A. H., Mladinic, A., & Otto, S. (1994). Cognitive and affective bases of attitudes toward social groups and social policies. *Journal of Experimental Social Psychology*, *30*(2), 113–137.

Fazio, R. H. (1986). How do attitudes guide behavior? In R. M. Sorrentino, & E. T. Higgins (Eds.), *Handbook of motivation and cognition: Foundations of social behavior* (pp. 204–243). New York: Guilford Press.

Greenwald, A. G., & Banaji, M. R. (1995). Implicit social cognition: Attitudes, self-esteem, and stereotypes. *Psychological Review*, *102*(1), 4–27.

Haddock, G., & Zanna, M. P. (1998). Assessing the impact of affective and cognitive information in predicting attitudes toward capital punishment. *Law and Human Behavior*, *22*(3), 325–339.

Hofmann, W., Gawronski, B., Gschwendner, T., Le, H., & Schmitt, M. (2005). A meta-analysis of the correlation between the Implicit Association Test and explicit self-report measures. *Personality and Social Psychology Bulletin*, *31*(1), 1369–1385.

Katz, D. (1960). The functional approach to the study of attitudes. *Public Opinion Quarterly*, *24*(2), 163–204.

Kothandapani, V. (1971). Validation of feeling, belief, and intention to act as three components of attitude and their contribution to prediction of contraceptive behavior. *Journal of Personality and Social Psychology*, *19*(3), 321–333.

Osgood, C. E., Suci, G. J., & Tannenbaum, P. H. (1957). *The measurement of meaning*. Urbana, IL: University of Illinois Press.

Ostrom, T. M. (1968). The emergence of attitude theory: 1930–1950. In A. G. Greenwald, T. C. Brock, & T. M. Ostrom (Eds.), *Psychological foundations of attitudes* (pp. 1–32). New York: Academic Press.

Ostrom, T. M. (1969). The relationship between the affective, behavioral, and cognitive components of attitude. *Journal of Experimental Social Psychology*, *5*(1), 12–30.

Rosenberg, M. J., & Hovland, C. I. (1960). Cognitive, affective, and behavioral components of attitude. In M. J. Rosenberg, C. I. Hovland, W. J. McGuire, R. P. Abelson, & J. W. Brehm (Eds.), *Attitude organization and change: An analysis of consistency among attitude components* (pp. 1–14). New Haven, CT: Yale University Press.

Sarnoff, I. (1960). Psychoanalytic theory and social attitudes. *Public Opinion Quarterly*, *24*(2), 251–279.

Sherif, M. (1960). Some needed concepts in the study of social attitudes. In J. Peatman, & E. Hartley (Eds.), *Festschrift for Gardner Murphy* (pp. 194–213). New York: Harper & Row.

Stangor, C., Sullivan, L. A., & Ford, T. E. (1991). Affective and cognitive determinants of prejudice. *Social Cognition*, *9*(4), 359–380.

Thomas, W. I., & Znaniecki, F. (1918). *The Polish peasant in Europe and America*. Boston: Richard G. Badger.

Verplanken, B., Hofstee, G., & Janssen, H. J. W. (1998). Accessibility of affective versus cognitive components of attitudes. *European Journal of Social Psychology*, *28*(1), 23–35.

Wicker, A. W. (1969). Attitudes versus actions: The relationship of verbal and overt behavioral responses to attitude objects. *Journal of Social Issues*, *25*(4), 41–78.

Wilson, T. D., & Hodges, S. D. (1992). Attitudes as temporary constructions. In L. L. Martin, & A. Tesser (Eds.), *The construction of social judgments* (pp. 37–65). Hillsdale, NJ: Lawrence Erlbaum Associates.

Zanna, M. P., & Rempel, J. K. (1988). Attitudes: A new look at an old concept. In D. Bar-Tal & A. W. Kruglanski (Eds.), *The social psychology of knowledge* (pp. 315–334). Cambridge: Cambridge University Press.

Chapter 2

Properties of Attitudes

Attitudes are associations between a given object and its evaluation, stored in memory, and as such have an *intra-attitudinal structure*. However, they are not "islands" of unrelated knowledge. Attitudes are also elements of our existing knowledge structures, including those linked to other attitudes. Therefore, they can also be analysed from the perspective of an *inter-attitudinal structure*. Such a structure can be organised, for example, based on ideology, which unites attitudes towards various political objects (see Converse, 1964; Cwalina & Falkowski, 2022).

The main defining characteristic of attitudes is their evaluative dimension, which is a continuum from negative to positive reactions to an object. However, understanding attitudes solely through this single dimension is insufficient and inadequate to explain their significance for our functioning: when they influence our behaviour, and when their influence is limited or absent. Therefore, analyses of intra-attitudinal structure aim to determine both how attitudes are represented in memory and the properties of this structure. The results of these analyses have allowed the identification of many such properties of attitudes.

2.1 The Internal Structure of Attitudes

If we define attitudes towards an object as a point on an evaluative continuum, we can ask about its scope. More precisely, this question asks whether the knowledge structure associated with the evaluation of an object includes beliefs about it and expectations about it, some of which are positive and some of which are negative, or whether all beliefs and expectations are exclusively positive or exclusively negative. In other words, this question asks whether an attitude has a **bipolar** or **unipolar structure** (Pratkanis & Greenwald, 1989). A bipolar structure does not mean that beliefs are always contradictory, but only that there are some that can be considered "for" and others that can be considered "against." Of course, the structure of an attitude can vary from person to person, which Hepler and Albarracín (2013, p. 1060) refer to as the

DOI: 10.4324/9781003589174-3

Bipolar attitudes. Attitudes in which the knowledge structure associated with the evaluation of an object includes beliefs about it and expectations about it, some of which are positive and some of which are negative.

Unipolar attitudes. Attitudes in which the knowledge structure associated with the evaluation of an object includes beliefs and expectations about it which are exclusively positive or exclusively negative.

Dispositional attitude. An individual difference in the general tendency to like versus dislike stimulation.

dispositional attitude, understood as "an individual difference in the general tendency to like versus dislike stimulation." However, the structure of an attitude also depends on its object. Unipolar attitudes most often concern objects that are not highly controversial (e.g., attitudes towards one's favourite football club or music band). Furthermore, if the attitudes of an individual's group (e.g., supporters of a political party) are strongly positive (negative) towards a given object, the individual's attitudes will also tend to fall along a part of an evaluative continuum, one of whose extremes is the neutral point. Whether a given attitude is bipolar or unipolar influences both how the attitude and its components are organised in memory and how people react to new information about the object and how the attitude may change. Pratkanis and Greenwald (1989) argue that, among other things, bipolar attitudes are more resistant to persuasion attempts than unipolar ones because they are more complex and therefore elicit counterarguments to opposing information.

One of the key properties of attitudes is their persistence. On the one hand, and historically, attitudes are considered global evaluations of an object stored in memory, which can be retrieved whenever the object appears. An alternative view is to treat attitudes as **temporary constructions** (e.g., Schwarz & Bohner, 2001; Wilson & Hodges, 1992). In this view, attitudes are assumed to be formed when an evaluative judgement is needed (as when someone asks what we think about a given object, e.g., aliens contacting humans). Fabrigar et al. (2019) distinguish between strong and weak versions of the constructivist approach. According to them, the strong version, which assumes that all attitudes are temporary, contradicts research findings and our own experience. It is unlikely that with repeated exposure to the same objects, we will evaluate their goodness or badness each time as if we were seeing them for the first time. It is not the case that one time we accept abortion as permissible in all circumstances, and another time that there are no justifications that would make abortion permissible, etc. The weak version of the approach to **attitudes as temporary constructions** assumes, instead, that they are formed in this way when global evaluations are not well-developed (i.e., their associations with the object are weak). Therefore, it is not the case that attitudes are either enduring or temporary, but rather that they lie at some point on a continuum between these extremes, and the precise point depends on their structural properties. This perspective, according to Fabrigar et al. (2019), is not inconsistent with the dominant view of **attitudes as general evaluations stored in memory**, which are sometimes created or updated based on new information or one's own knowledge. The durability of attitudes does not imply their rigidity.

Attitudes as general evaluations stored in memory. Attitudes are general, relatively enduring evaluations stored in memory which can be retrieved whenever the object appears.

Attitudes as temporary constructions. Attitudes are assumed to be formed when an evaluative judgement is needed (as when someone asks what we think about a given object).

Attitude strength. Strong attitudes are characterised by being relatively resistant to change and exerting a significant influence on information processing and individual behaviour.

Some attitudes are enduring and impactful, while others are rather weak, with minimal consequences. Therefore, one of the key properties of attitudes is their **strength** (Howe & Krosnick, 2017). Strong attitudes are characterised by being relatively resistant to change and exerting a significant influence on information processing and individual behaviour. Research on **attitude strength** has identified many more specific features, generally suggesting that attitude strength is a multidimensional construct (e.g., Krosnick et al., 1993; Pomerantz et al., 1995).

First, a strong attitude is one to which an individual attaches great **importance**. This importance may stem from the fact that the attitude object may relate to the individual's core values (e.g., a person supports abortion because of the value of freedom of choice). Self-interest may also underlie attitude importance. For example, a positive evaluation of possessing exclusive goods may be associated with a person's high status and lifestyle. An attitude may also be important because it aligns with the beliefs of the group with which the individual identifies. The second characteristic of a strong attitude is its **accessibility**, or the strength of the link between the evaluation and the object in memory. Attitudes that are chronically accessible will be activated more likely or automatically (spontaneously) upon encountering the attitude object (Fazio, 2007).

Attitude accessibility. The strength of the link between the evaluation and the object in memory. Chronically accessible attitudes are activated more likely or automatically (spontaneously) upon encountering the attitude object.

Attitudinal ambivalence. Positive and negative, conflicting evaluations of the attitude object are activated simultaneously.

Affective-cognitive consistency of attitude. Knowledge about an object is consistent with the individual's feelings about it.

The third characteristic of strong attitudes is their **intensity**, which manifests itself in the powerful emotions evoked upon contact with a given object. The stronger these emotions, the greater the attitude intensity. Another aspect of attitude strength is **extremity**, operationalised as the distance of an individual's attitude from the midpoint of the favourable–unfavourable dimension. In other words, it is the degree to which a person likes (or loves) or dislikes (or hates) a given object. Fifth, attitudes can be characterised by varying degrees of **certainty**. This characteristic refers to an individual's confidence that they know the object well and that their evaluation of it is accurate and correct. It should be emphasised, however, that people are typically overconfident in their judgements and the accuracy of their knowledge (Einhorn & Hogarth, 1978). Attitude strength also depends on the depth and consistency of **knowledge** or information a person has about a given object and the extent to which this knowledge is the result of **elaboration**, self-generated reflections, and self-focused reflections.

A strong attitude is also one that has significant **affective-cognitive consistency**. In this case, knowledge about an object is consistent with the individual's feelings about it (e.g., "I like apples because they are very healthy"). This feature is somewhat related to the last of the basic characteristics of attitude strength – **ambivalence**. Attitudinal ambivalence occurs when positive and negative reactions to an attitude object are activated simultaneously. Thus, it can occur when conflicting evaluations of the object concern the same dimension (e.g., opposing feelings or contradictory beliefs), but also when they are cross-dimensional (as in the case of affective-cognitive inconsistency: "I love chocolate, but it has a lot of calories") (see Fabrigar et al., 2019). However, ambivalence is not always experienced as discomfort. According to van Harreveld et al. (2009), it is experienced as unpleasant only when the positive and negative elements of the attitude are both salient and accessible, as for example when someone requires us to take a specific position and stand on one side of a conflict or dispute.

All of these traits constitute different aspects of attitude strength. Although some of these dimensions are highly correlated, they also exhibit significant differences (Krosnick et al., 1993). For example, Luttrell et al. (2016), using functional magnetic resonance imaging (fMRI), demonstrated that although certainty and ambivalence are related, different brain regions are uniquely responsive to each. Furthermore, although all of these traits influence the intention to behave consistently with attitudes, their impact on other aspects of our functioning may be different. Pomerantz et al. (1995) found that, for example, while attitude extremity was associated with increased selective elaboration, selective judgements, and attitude polarisation, attitude importance, in turn, decreased selective elaboration and increased information seeking. A significant effect of individual differences was also found for individual traits of attitude strength. Britt et al. (2009) found that attitude certainty and extremity were positively associated with the level of the need to evaluate (i.e., a chronic tendency to evaluate objects as good or bad) and the need for affect (i.e., the need to seek out or avoid emotionally arousing situations), while dogmatism (i.e., a relatively closed cognitive system of beliefs about reality) was a predictor of attitude importance.

2.2 The Functions of an Attitude

But, why do we need these evaluations? One cannot pursue the study of attitudes far without inquiring about their functions for the individual. The functional approach to attitudes assumes that people hold and express particular attitudes because they derive psychological benefit from doing so; however, the type of benefit varies among individuals. Then, it is the attempt to understand the reasons people hold the attitudes they do (Katz, 1960; Smith et al., 1956). These reasons lie in the sphere of psychological motivations, and that is why attitude activation is dependent upon the arousal of some need in the individual, or the occurrence of some relevant cue in the environment (Maio et al., 2004). In other words, attitudes should be understood according to the psychological needs they meet – the functions they serve. However, Fabrigar et al. (2019) argue that attitudes may serve different functions also because they are associated with different types of information. Thus, just as attitude-relevant information can vary in affective, cognitive, or behavioural content, it can also vary in functional content. From this perspective, one can refer to attitude functions as a structural property.

Although no exhaustive list of functions was ever agreed upon, some major psychological needs were consistently assumed to be met by attitudes. In his classic work, Katz (1960) distinguishes four functions of attitudes

> **Instrumental (or utilitarian) function of attitudes**. Attitudes help an individual maximise rewards and minimise punishments from the environment: approach objects that are evaluated positively and avoid those evaluated negatively.
>
> **Knowledge function of attitudes**. Attitudes help organise and categorise the world in a meaningful and consistent fashion, providing order, clarity, and stability in one's frame of reference, or the worldview.

that he considers basic and universal: instrumental or utilitarian, knowledge, ego-defensive, and value-expressive. The first of these is the **instrumental or utilitarian function**. Its essence is that attitudes help an individual maximise rewards and minimise punishments from the environment: approach objects that are evaluated positively and avoid those evaluated negatively. Therefore, the dynamics of attitude formation with respect to the instrumental function depend on the current or past perceptions of the usefulness of the attitude object for a given person. People approach individuals they find attractive, eat foods that look fresh and tasty, and if they consider AI a useful tool, they use it in corporate correspondence. However, people avoid contact with groups against which they are prejudiced, or they do not buy products from a country that is famous for producing crap. From this perspective, to activate an attitude it is necessary to arouse their relevant need states and the occurrence of the cues associated with the content of the attitude. In contrast, an attitude that serves an instrumental function is likely to change when it and its related activities no longer provide the gratifications previously achieved, or when the individual's level of aspiration has been raised.

The second function of attitudes distinguished by Katz (1960) is the **knowledge function**. Attitudes help organise and categorise the world in a meaningful and consistent fashion, providing order, clarity, and stability in one's frame of reference, or the worldview. This function is related to seek knowledge to give meaning to what would otherwise be an unorganised chaotic universe. Attitudes provide just such a simple structure for organising the environment and coping with it.

In another classic functional approach, Smith et al. (1956) do not distinguish between the utilitarian and knowledge functions but describe their key characteristics as an **object appraisal function**. This function captures the fact that we organise for action the objects of the world according to our major interests and ongoing concerns. Based on the above analyses, Pratkanis and Greenwald (1989; Pratkanis, 1988) argue that attitudes serve two functions: *heuristic* and *schematic*. Attitudes, understood as an evaluative summary of past experience and knowledge about a social object, can operate as heuristics that are used as an implicit theory to interpret and explain the social world. The knowledge structure supporting an evaluation serves a schematic function. It organises and guides memory for events and complex action towards an object. Moreover, an attitude is held in service of the most important attitude object – the self, and therefore it is used to define and maintain self-worth.

Ego-defensive function of attitudes. Attitudes protect a person from unwanted thoughts and beliefs about the self or the harsh realities in her external world.

The third function of attitudes distinguished by Katz (1960) is the **ego-defensive function** in which the person protects herself from unwanted thoughts and beliefs about the self or the harsh realities in her external world. This function is also referred to as *externalisation* (Smith et al., 1956). Attitudes that help to protect the individual from anxiety generated by an intrapsychic conflict or from facing up to external dangers are elicited by any form of threat to the ego (Hart, 2014). The threat may be external, such as a highly competitive situation, failure, or hearing an insulting comment about yourself. Activation of the ego-defensive attitude may also be the result of the encouragement given to its expression by some form of social support. For example, an important element of many Domestic Violence Intervention Programmes is the focus on changing the attitudes and behaviours of victims of violence related to issues of power and control and towards offenders (Campbell et al., 2024).

The expression of ego-defensive attitudes may also be internally conditioned, for example, by the anxiety experienced by the individual (Katz, 1960). Terror management theory (TMT) suggests that our most vile attitudes and actions towards other groups stem from a fear we cannot fully cope with or comprehend – the fear of our own mortality (e.g., Pyszczynski et al., 1999). TMT posits that in order to manage the potential terror engendered by the awareness of mortality, people must sustain (a) faith in a cultural worldview that imbues reality with order, meaning, and permanence and provides paths to literal and/or symbolic immortality for those who meet prescribed standards of value and (b) belief that they are meeting standards of value prescribed in the culture at large (e.g., the feeling of self-esteem). A variety of studies have examined whether reminders of mortality increase negative reactions to others who subscribe to different worldviews. For example, Greenberg et al. (1990) showed that mortality salience increased American Christian students' liking of a fellow Christian student and increased their disliking of a Jewish student and attributing to him more negative stereotypic traits (e.g., cheap). In turn, Schimel et al. (1999) found that mortality salience led Americans to view Germans in more stereotypic ways (e.g., as being highly orderly and rigid in their ways), although this group was not particularly disliked by the population of American college students participating in the study.

> **Value-expressive function of attitudes**. The individual derives satisfaction from expressing attitudes appropriate to her personal values and to her self-concept.

The last function described by Katz (1960) is the **value-expressive function** of attitudes, which is manifested in the fact that the individual derives satisfaction from expressing attitudes appropriate to her personal values and to her self-concept (Katz, 1960). For a value to enter into a person's attitudes on a topic there are at least two necessary conditions: the scope of the value must be broad enough to apply to the topic, and the information available to the person must contain at least some basis for engaging his value. By expressing values important to one's self-concept, a person establishes self-identity and confirms her notion of the sort of person she sees herself to be. This has no connection with whether expressing such an attitude is associated with gaining social recognition or any material (e.g., monetary) rewards.

Attitudes also can mediate one's interpersonal relations, fulfilling the function of **social adjustment** (Smith et al., 1956). This function is based on needs to be accepted by others in one's own immediate social environment and to signal their membership in or identification with particular social groups or categories (Shavitt, 1989).

In his neofunctional theory of attitudes, Herek (1986) proposed to organise all these attitude functions based on the distinction between pleasure or displeasure caused by the attitude object (i.e., utilitarian and knowledge functions) and that resulting from the expression of the attitude (i.e., ego-defensive, value-expressive, and social adjustment functions). When a high level of value is attached to the attitude object itself but little value is associated with expressing the attitude, the attitude serves an evaluative function. When a high level of value is attached to the attitude's expression but not to the object, the attitude serves one of the expressive functions. When neither valence is high, the attitude is nonfunctional; such attitudes are not strongly held and can be easily changed. Finally, attitudes serving both kinds of function are referred to as complex (e.g., intergroup attitudes are likely to serve both evaluative and expressive functions).

However, the functional approach to attitudes also emphasises that the influences in the real world are not as a rule directed towards a single type of motivation (Maio et al., 2004). Contact with other peoples, experience in foreign cultures, group pressures, group discussion, and decisions are all global variables, and they represent combinations of forces (Katz, 1960). Furthermore, each of these functions can play themselves out in individual or social situations. Tesser (1993) emphasises that regardless of the function served, one might expect that others who support one's ego-defensive attitudes would not be threatening. Similar others are likely to validate one's interpretation of the situation, confirm one's self-view, and provide easy or uncostly interaction.

Further Reading

Fabrigar, L. R., MacDonald, T. K., & Wegener, D. T. (2019). The origins and structure of attitudes. In D. Albarracín, & B. T. Johnson (Eds.), *Handbook of attitudes, Volume 1: Basic principles* (pp. 109–157). New York: Routledge.

References

Britt, T. W., Millard, M. R., Sundareswaran, P. T., & Moore, D. (2009). Personality variables predict strength-related attitude dimensions across objects. *Journal of Personality, 77*(3), 859–882.

Campbell, J. K., Nicolla, S., Weissman, D. M., & Moracco, K. E. (2024). The uptake and measurement of alternative approaches to Domestic Violence Intervention Programs: A scoping review. *Trauma, Violence, & Abuse, 25*(4), 3269–3284.

Converse, P. E. (1964). The nature of belief systems in mass public. In D. E. Apter (Ed.), *Ideology and discontent,* (pp. 206–261). New York: The Free Press of Glencoe.

Cwalina, W., & Falkowski, A. (2022). Political marketing from an ideological marketing perspective. In B. I. Newman, & T. P. Newman (Eds.), *A research agenda for political marketing* (pp. 15–49). Cheltenham: Edward Elgar Publishing.

Einhorn, H. J., & Hogarth, R. M. (1978). Confidence in judgment: Persistence of the illusion of validity. *Psychological Review, 85*(5), 395–416.

Fabrigar, L. R., MacDonald, T. K., & Wegener, D. T. (2019). The origins and structure of attitudes. In D. Albarracín, & B. T. Johnson (Eds.), *Handbook of attitudes, Volume 1: Basic principles* (pp. 109–157). New York: Routledge.

Fazio, R. H. (2007). Attitudes as object-evaluation associations of varying strength. *Social Cognition, 25*(5), 603–637.

Greenberg, J., Pyszczynski, T., Solomon, S., Rosenblatt, A., Veeder, M., Kirkland, S., & Lyon, D. (1990). Evidence for terror management theory II: The effects of mortality salience on reactions to those who threaten or bolster the cultural worldview. *Journal of Personality and Social Psychology, 58*(2), 308–318.

Hart, J. (2014). Toward an integrative theory of psychological defense. *Perspectives on Psychological Science, 9*(1), 19–39.

Hepler, J., & Albarracín, D. (2013). Attitudes without objects: Evidence for a dispositional attitude, its measurement, and its consequences. *Journal of Personality and Social Psychology, 104*(6), 1060–1076.

Herek, G. M. (1986). The instrumentality of attitudes: Toward a neofunctional theory. *Journal of Social Issues, 42*(2), 99–114.

Howe, L. C., & Krosnick, J. A. (2017). Attitude strength. *Annual Review of Psychology, 68,* 327–351.

Katz, D. (1960). The functional approach to the study of attitudes. *Public Opinion Quarterly, 24*(2), 163–204.

Krosnick, J. A., Boninger, D. S., Chuang, Y. C., Berent, M. K., & Carnot, C. G. (1993). Attitude strength: One construct or many related constructs? *Journal of Personality and Social Psychology, 65*(6), 1132–1151.

Luttrell, A., Stillman, P. E., Hasinski, A. E., & Cunningham, W. A. (2016). Neural dissociations in attitude strength: Distinct regions of cingulate cortex track ambivalence and certainty. *Journal of Experimental Psychology: General, 145*(4), 419–433.

Maio, G. R., Esses, V. M., Arnold, H. K., & Olson, J. M. (2004). The function–structure model of attitudes: Incorporating the need for affect. In G. Haddock, & G. R. Maio (Eds.), *Contemporary perspectives on the psychology of attitudes* (pp. 9–33). Hove: Psychology Press.

Pomerantz, E. M., Chaiken, S., & Tordesillas, R. S. (1995). Attitude strength and resistance processes. *Journal of Personality and Social Psychology, 69*(3), 408–419.

Pratkanis, A. R. (1988). The attitude heuristic and selective fact identification. *British Journal of Social Psychology, 27*(3), 257–263.

Pratkanis, A. R., & Greenwald, A. G. (1989). A sociocognitive model of attitude structure and function. In L. Berkowitz (Ed.), *Advances in experimental social psychology* (Vol. 22, pp. 245–285). San Diego, CA: Academic Press.

Pyszczynski, T., Greenberg, J., & Solomon, S. (1999). A dual-process model of defense against conscious and unconscious death-related thoughts: An extension of terror management theory. *Psychological Review, 106*(4), 835–845.

Schimel, J., Simon, L., Greenberg, J., Pyszczynski, T., Solomon, S., Waxmonsky, J., & Arndt, J. (1999). Stereotypes and terror management: Evidence that mortality salience enhances stereotypic thinking and preferences. *Journal of Personality and Social Psychology, 77*(5), 905–926.

Schwarz, N., & Bohner, G. (2001). The construction of attitudes. In A. Tesser & N. Schwarz (Eds.), *Blackwell handbook of social psychology: Intraindividual processes* (pp. 436–457). Malden, MA: Blackwell Publishers.

Shavitt, S. (1989). Operationalizing functional theories of attitude. In A. R. Pratkanis, S. J. Breckler, & A. G. Greenwald (Eds.), *Attitude structure and function* (pp. 311–337). Hillsdale, NJ: Lawrence Erlbaum Associates, Inc.

Smith, M. B., Bruner, J. S., & White, R. W. (1956). *Opinions and personality.* New York: John Wiley & Sons.

Tesser, A. (1993). The importance of heritability in psychological research: The case of attitudes. *Psychological Review, 100*(1), 129–142.

van Harreveld, F., van der Pligt, J., & de Liver, Y. N. (2009). The agony of ambivalence and ways to resolve it: Introducing the MAID model. *Personality and Social Psychology Review, 13*(1), 45–61.

Wilson, T. D., & Hodges, S. D. (1992). Attitudes as temporary constructions. In L. L. Martin, & A. Tesser (Eds.), *The construction of social judgments* (pp. 37–65). Hillsdale, NJ: Lawrence Erlbaum Associates.

Chapter 3

Attitude Formation

The definition of an attitude implies that it can apply to any object that can be thought of. This does not mean, however, that an attitude is formed towards every object encountered (Fazio et al., 1983–1984). In other words, not every contact with an object initiates the process of attitude formation towards it.

When psychologists try to determine the origins of a psychological phenomenon, such as a personality trait or ability, they usually try to determine to what extent the phenomenon is genetically determined and to what extent it is the result of environmental or social influences. This also applies to the question of the origins of attitudes. Although the dominant view is that attitudes are acquired and shaped socially, there is also some evidence that they may have a genetic basis.

3.1 Genetic Basis of Attitudes

Heredity and environment are so closely intertwined that they cannot be completely separated. Genetic factors influence an organism's response to a given environment, so the final product is inevitably a combination of biological and empirical factors. Thus, according to Olson et al. (2001, pp. 845–846), "Asking how much a particular individual's attitudes or traits are due to heredity versus the environment is nonsensical, just like asking whether a leaky basement is caused more by the crack in the foundation or the water outside." Genetic effects are also environmental in nature because they occur in a specific environment, and environmental effects are also genetic in nature because they are mediated by biological processes. Nevertheless, despite their interrelationship, it is possible to estimate the extent to which differences between individuals in an attitude or trait can be attributed to genetic or environmental factors.

Tesser (1993) indicates a number of mechanisms by which more directly heritable physical differences might play themselves out in specific attitudes in a particular environment. These are, first, sensory structures. Genetic differences in such structures as taste, hearing, and sensitivity

DOI: 10.4324/9781003589174-4

to touch could affect, for example, attitudes towards food, loud music, preferences for lovemaking practices, and so forth. Similarly, genetic differences in temperament and activity level may have an impact on attitudes towards various free-time pursuits and career options.

Body chemistry (e.g., hormones) also has profound effects on behaviour and preferences. For example, Coates and Herbert (2008) sampled, under real working conditions, endogenous steroids (testosterone and cortisol) from a group of male traders in the City of London. They found that elevated levels of steroids may shift attitudes and preference to risk, as well as affect traders' profitability. In another area, political attitudes and beliefs, Durante et al. (2013) tested how fertility influenced women's politics, religiosity, and voting in the 2012 U.S. presidential election. They found that ovulation had drastically different effects on single women and women in committed relationships. Ovulation led single women to become more liberal, less religious, and more likely to vote for Barack Obama. In contrast, ovulation led women in committed relationships to become more conservative, more religious, and more likely to vote for Mitt Romney. In addition, ovulation-induced changes in political orientation mediated women's voting behaviour.

The most convincing evidence for the genetic determinants of attitudes is that provided by twin studies. Estimates of genetic influence are labelled **heritability coefficient** (h^2). Heritability coefficients of up to 0.5 are interpreted as meaning that 50% of the variation in a given trait (including attitude) between individuals belonging to a population can be attributed to the genetic variance of that population. Then, heritability coefficients do not indicate the extent to which characteristics are genetically caused. Rather, they indicate the extent to which variation on the characteristic in the sample is attributable to genetic differences. Any genetic or environmental influences that apply uniformly to all members of the sample will not be reflected in this statistic (Olson et al., 2001).

Olson et al. (2001) analysed the genetic basis of individual differences in 30 attitudes in a survey of pairs of monozygotic twins and same-sex dizygotic twins from the Canadian population. Participants' attitudes towards controversial issues (e.g., abortion on demand, or voluntary euthanasia), personal activities (e.g., playing bingo, or exercising), and social issues (e.g., capitalism, or religion) were measured. Their analyses indicated that six of the nine general attitudes (e.g., towards the preservation of life, or towards athleticism) yielded significant heritability coefficients (with a median h^2

Heritability coefficient (h^2). The proportion of variance in a trait within a population that is attributed to genetic differences.

of 0.41). However, the most significant predictor of variability in attitude scores was variation in experiences that were unique to individual members of twin pairs (i.e., nonshared environmental factors).

In political domain, Bell et al. (2018) examined individual differences in liberalism/conservatism in a German sample that included twins, their parents, and their spouses and incorporated both self- and peer reports. They found that based solely on the self-reports of family members, approximately 38.5% of the variance in liberalism/conservatism was attributable to additive genetic effects (h^2). In this context, however, it should be emphasised that research on genetic determinants in relation to political attitudes and behaviour (so-called "genopolitics") is subject to strong criticism (see Charney & English, 2012).

To sum up, as Chabris et al. (2015, p. 310) strongly emphasise, "it is mistaken to believe that there might be a gene 'for' one complex trait or another." Then, how an individual looks or behaves results from the full range of gene expression evoked in a particular environment. According to Fausto-Sterling (1997), the most common fallacy encountered in discussions about the genetic basis of behaviour is the presumption that individuals have constant environments, and that, in the absence of empirical measures, one can predict for any or all environments, the phenotype produced by a particular gene.

Although people possess certain innate dispositions that may influence the attitudes they develop later in life, external influences undoubtedly play a large role in shaping attitudes. Researchers have identified several different processes through which associations between an attitude object and an evaluation may be acquired, occurring both with and without awareness.

3.2 Mere Exposure

What are the chances you'll like a song by an unknown band you've never heard before? And when you hear it a second, third, fourth time... It turns out that often, mere contact with an object can make it attractive. This phenomenon is called the **mere exposure** effect (Zajonc, 1968). It refers to the fact that mere repeated exposure of the individual to a stimulus is a sufficient condition for the enhancement of his attitude towards it. As defined by Zajonc (1968, p. 1), "by 'mere exposure' is meant a condition which just makes the given stimulus accessible to the individual's perception." However, recognising the stimulus as previously presented is not a necessary condition for this effect to occur.

Mere exposure. Mere repeated exposure of the individual to a stimulus is a sufficient condition for the enhancement of his attitude towards it.

Zajonc (1980) explains this effect by arguing that the feelings that accompany all cognitive processes are primary to them and that emotions originate from a parallel, separate, and partially independent system in the body. Affective reactions are inevitable. Unlike cognitive judgements about the objective characteristics of stimuli, affective reactions accompanying these stimuli cannot be arbitrarily influenced. They usually occur regardless of whether one intends them to. Furthermore, affective reactions can be separated from the content. In many cases, a person cannot recall the content of a given event, but they can easily recall the emotions it evoked.

Another mechanism underlying the mere exposure effect is indicated by Lee (2001). In the approach she calls an **uncertainty reduction view**, she assumes that individuals prefer stimuli that are familiar and predictable and that perceptual fluency reflects learning, and therefore uncertainty reduction, even in the absence of recognition, which leads to an increase in liking. Therefore, when individuals recognise a stimulus (correctly or otherwise) as one that has been previously presented, a sense of familiarity results in increased liking for the stimulus, even at times when familiarity may not be justified. This view thus predicts that old stimuli are preferred to new stimuli and stimuli thought to be presented are preferred to stimuli thought to be not presented. Hence, old-presented stimuli should be most preferred, whereas new-not-presented stimuli should be least preferred.

Bornstein (1989) reviewed 208 studies that used a variety of stimuli (e.g., nonsense words, ideographs, geometric shapes, photographs) and found that there was good evidence that more exposures to a stimulus made it more likeable. However, the mere exposure effect has some limitations. First, the stimulus should initially be neutral or at least non-aversive, because repeated presentation of disliked stimuli increases aversion. Second, the effect of mere exposure is stronger when the stimulus presentation times are short (including subliminal exposure) and when the stimuli are presented in a varied rather than homogeneous sequence. Third, the curve between exposure frequency and affect peaks with a relatively small number of presentations. After approximately 10–20 exposures, affect ceases to increase further (i.e., the curve becomes "flat"). Fourth, the effect of mere exposure increases with increasing time intervals between stimulus exposure and its evaluation. Fifth, the effect of mere exposure becomes stronger with increasing age of the participants. And sixth, the effect is more pronounced for more complex stimuli than for simple ones.

3.3 Classical Conditioning

Sometimes, simply being exposed to previously neutral stimuli is enough to develop a liking for them. However, we may also begin to like something because exposure to a given stimulus was associated with experiencing positive emotion elicited by other sources. We may also begin to dislike something because it was associated with aversive stimuli.

Attitudes can be considered learned implicit responses (Staats et al., 1980). All objects in an environment elicit responses from an organism. For example, food objects when put in the mouth elicit responses of tasting, chewing, and swallowing; a ball in the hand elicits certain other responses: grasping, throwing, etc. Some of these responses are dependent for their elicitation upon the actual sensory presence of the object for their occurrence, but others can occur without the object being present. These detachable responses may become conditioned to the verbal stimuli with which the object is repeatedly paired. Thus a word comes to elicit in an individual part of the response which the object itself elicits. It is suggested that it is, at least in part, through language conditioning that attitudes are developed and changed in everyday life.

Staats and Staats (1958) applied a **classical conditioning** formulation to form attitudes towards national names. Two types of stimuli were used: national names that were presented by slide projection on a screen (conditioned stimulus; CS) and words that were presented orally by the experimenter (conditioned stimulus; US), which the participant had to immediately repeat aloud. Ostensibly, participants' task was to separately learn the verbal stimuli simultaneously presented in the two different ways. Six national names were used as the CS's: German, Swedish, Italian, French, Dutch, and Greek. The names were each visually presented 18 times in random order, each time with a different auditorily presented word. Then, there were 18 conditioning trials, and CS names were never paired with US words more than once. Moreover, the CS names, Swedish and Dutch, were always paired with US words with evaluative meaning, while the other four CS names were paired with words which had no systematic meaning (e.g., chair, with, twelve). For half of the participants, Dutch was paired with different words which had positive evaluative meaning (e.g., gift, sacred, happy), and Swedish was paired with words which had negative evaluative meaning (e.g., bitter, ugly, failure). For the other half of the participants, the order of Dutch and Swedish was reversed. Once the conditioning phase was completed, participants were asked to rate each country name on a scale from pleasant to unpleasant. The results showed that

Classical conditioning. The process of an initially neutral stimulus acquiring meaning as a result of its co-occurrence with a stimulus that elicits a positive or negative emotional response.

meaning responses were conditioned to the names without participants' awareness. Attitudes towards the country name were significantly more positive when it was paired with a positive word than a negative word. Staats and Staats (1958) emphasise that the results of the experiment do not directly show that the individual's reaction to the object (e.g., a person of Dutch nationality) changed, but that the attitudinal response to the signs, the national names themselves, was conditioned. Nevertheless, this reaction may, over time, generalise and lead to the development of stereotypes.

Human attitudes, then, can be classically conditioned. Due to the dearth of attitude-relevant information about a novel stimulus and too little or no preexposure, Cacioppo et al. (1992) state that classical conditioning should be a more powerful determinant of attitude formation than attitude change. However, the issue of classical conditioning should be approached with some caution. Rescorla (1988) shows that traditional descriptions of Pavlovian (classical) conditioning as the acquired ability of one stimulus to evoke the original response to another because of their pairing are inadequate in light of current understanding. Instead, conditioning is now described as the learning of relationships among events so as to allow the organism to represent its environment and anticipate events that may occur within it.

3.4 Evaluative Conditioning

Evaluative conditioning refers to changes in liking that are due to the pairing of stimuli and describes how individuals use ecological regularities to inform their attitudes (De Houwer, 2007). In a prototypical procedure used to demonstrate evaluative conditioning, neutral conditioned stimuli (CS) such as objects, faces, or brand names are repeatedly shown with liked or disliked unconditioned stimuli (US) such as affective pictures, words, or scents. Notwithstanding earlier controversy, it is a well-established finding that adult participants evaluate CS paired with liked US more favourably after conditioning as compared to CS paired with disliked US (Hofmann et al., 2010).

Unlike in classical conditioning research, the formerly neutral CS in an evaluative conditioning paradigm does not acquire a predictive value but merely acquires the affective qualities of the liked or disliked US. Then, whereas Pavlovian conditioning can refer to a change in any type of response, evaluative conditioning concerns only

Evaluative conditioning. Attitude formation or change towards an object due to that object's mere co-occurrence with another valenced object or objects.

a change in the evaluative responses to the CS, that is, a change in the liking of the CS. This conditioning effect is usually explained by the formation of an association between the cognitive representation of the CS and the US; however, the mechanism by which it arises is extensively debated (see Hofmann et al., 2010; Walther et al., 2005). Furthermore, an evaluative conditioned attitude seems to be more robust than reactions in classical conditioning.

For example, Halbeisen et al. (2017) hypothesised that young children could use the regularities between neutral and affective stimuli to inform their attitudes. Consistent with that hypothesis, they obtained evidence for evaluative conditioning, that is, evidence for attitude formation that is due to the pairing of stimuli. Specifically, they found that three- to six-year-old children preferred CS (unknown cartoon characters in the first experiment, and fribbles in the second experiment) paired with liked US (puppy and ice cream, respectively) over CS paired with disliked US (spider and Labskaus, respectively).

Krosnick et al. (1992) found that pairing a subliminally presented affect-arousing slide with presentation of photos of a target person influenced subjects' attitudes towards the target person. When the target person was paired with positive affect, she was liked more and was seen as having more complimentary personality traits than when she was paired with negative affect. However, the subliminal slides did not shape all evaluative judgements about the target person equally. Beliefs about her physical attractiveness, which could be based on salient objective data, appeared to be less affected, although the results on this point were relatively weak. Nonetheless, these studies demonstrate that it is possible to like or dislike a person without knowing the correct reason for the attitude.

3.5 Operant Conditioning

Operant (or instrumental) conditioning, developed by Skinner (1953), is a learning process where behaviours are influenced by consequences. Positive reinforcement encourages a behaviour by adding a reward, while negative reinforcement strengthens it by removing an unpleasant stimulus. Punishment, in contrast, decreases a behaviour by introducing a negative consequence or removing a positive one. This learning mechanism also

> **Operant (or instrumental) conditioning.** A learning process where behaviours are influenced by consequences: actions that are followed by reinforcement (rewards or positive outcomes) are strengthened and more likely to be repeated, while actions followed by punishment or negative consequences are weakened and less likely to occur.

applies to the formation and consolidation of attitudes. However, the key point here is that reinforcement is social in nature: it is provided by other people. These may be peers, superiors at work, or authorities. However, such comments (positive or negative) may be normative or informative in nature (Deutsch & Gerard, 1955). On the one hand, reinforcement may come from the group and may signal to the individual that her attitudes are consistent with the prevailing norm within that group. Individuals adopt attitudes valued within their own group (that is, those valued by most of its members, especially by its leaders) to the extent that this group (especially as represented by its leaders and by higher-status subgroups) serves as a positive reference point for them (Newcomb, 1952). Furthermore, negative social attitudes towards one group lead to positive attitudes towards another, or vice versa. In this way, attitudes are doubly reinforced. In a community where certain attitudes are endorsed, the development of an individual's attitude is a function of how they relate to the group as a whole and to one or more reference groups.

On the other hand, reinforcement may inform and reassure the individual that her attitudes are "correct" and thus further strengthen them. For example, in an experiment conducted by Insko (1965) in Hawaii, the participants were asked in a supposed telephone survey to either agree or disagree with a series of statements regarding the creation of a Springtime Aloha Week. The statements, which were so phrased that agreement with one half and disagreement with the other half indicated a positive attitude, were assertions of opinion and not attitude. They did not say that the creation of a Springtime Aloha Week was good or bad but simply that it would lead to certain ends such as more tourist dollars or growing traffic congestion. Assistant experimenter reinforced responses, saying "good," indicating positive attitudes for half of the participants and responses indicating negative attitudes for the other half. After a week, the same participants, this time in class, were asked again to express their attitude towards the event. It was found that verbal reinforcement produced an effect on the telephone responses that carried over to the attitude questionnaire. Hildum and Brown (1956) also reported that saying "good" (but not "Mm–hmm") during a telephone interview was an effective reinforcer in shaping attitudes towards the fictitious the Harvard philosophy general education. These results suggest that verbal reinforcement can produce a genuine effect on attitude formation and not just a transitory effect upon interview responses.

3.6 Observational Learning

The behavioral repertoires which constitute an enduring part of a culture are to a large extent transmitted on the basis of repeated observation of behavior displayed by social models rather than by

> memory drums. While the learning process is essentially the same, the characteristics of the social transmitters and other interpersonal variables can greatly affect the rate, level, and types of responses that will be acquired observationally.
>
> (Bandura, 1965, p. 48)

A **vicarious (observational) learning** event is defined as one in which new responses are acquired or the characteristics of existing response repertoires are modified as a function of observing the behaviour of others (or "vicars") and its reinforcing consequences, without the modelled responses being overtly performed by the viewer during the exposure period (Bandura, 1965). Thus, the response of the other has the same or similar effect on the characteristics of the observer *as if* the observer had performed the response herself, thereby altering her response repertory (deCharms & Rosenbaum, 1960). This mode of response acquisition is treated as no-trial learning, since the observer does not engage in any overt responding trials although he may require multiple observational trials in order to reproduce the modelled stimuli accurately.

Attitudes are frequently established on the basis of modelled pairings in which the attributes of target persons and objects are associated by the model with verbal stimuli likely to evoke in the observer intense, emotional responses (Bandura, 1965). Given that the model's emotional behaviour is in the context of a particular stimulus situation, this stimulus situation should be able to elicit the relevant emotion in the observer. Thus the specific stimulus situation, or another similar stimulus situation, comes to be a positive or negative attitudinal object for the observer, depending on the nature of the model's emotional response (Kanekar, 1976).

One of the most intuitive situations in which observational learning, or modelling, occurs is the parent-child relationship. Parents may deliberately reinforce their children's expressions of attitudes they themselves approve of. However, they may also unintentionally influence their children's attitudes by providing them with a model. Numerous studies on political socialisation show that the family is the most important source of partisanship for children. Although early studies pointed to the father as the model for children's political attitudes (e.g., Iyengar,

Observational learning (modelling). New responses are acquired, or the characteristics of existing response repertoires are modified as a function of observing the behaviour of others, without the modelled responses being overtly performed by the viewer during the exposure period.

1976), a growing body of research demonstrates that a politically active mother can have a role-model effect, especially for their daughters (e.g., Gidengil et al., 2010). However, research also shows that daughters are less likely than sons to adopt their parents' rightist positions, while parent-son transmission is equally large on the left and the right (Van Ditmars, 2023).

The probability of modelling usually increases with model–observer similarity, along such dimensions as gender, age, or opinions. Hilmert et al. (2006) demonstrated that observing a model express liking for a piece of music induced more favourable opinions of the music (positive modelling) when the model was similar to the participant observer in relevant opinions, and more negative opinions (negative modelling) when the model was dissimilar to the participant in relevant opinions.

Not only can the verbal expression of attitudes by the model lead to observational learning in observers, but nonverbal signals also have the potential to create and spread attitudes towards others. In a series of studies, Skinner and Perry (2019) examined whether seeing one individual receive more cold, unfriendly nonverbal signals than another individual would lead to biases in favour of the target of more positive nonverbal signals (e.g., in one of the studies the television show's main character, Ally McBeal served as the expresser demonstrating nonverbal signals). Consistent with predictions, exposure to nonverbal bias in favour of one individual over another led participants to develop nonverbal signal-consistent explicit biases.

3.7 Acquiring Attitudes through Exploration

We also acquire attitudes through direct experience while exploring our social environment, but our exploration is selectively focused in directions we anticipate to be rewarding. In other words, we approach things we expect to be good and give pleasure, and avoid things we expect to be bad and give pain. This can lead us to identify sufficiently safe or rewarding experiences, albeit at the price of leaving some other potentially rewarding regions of our life space unexplored (Eiser, 2004). When we want to dine in a country whose cuisine we're unfamiliar with, a "safe" strategy might be to look for a restaurant serving dishes of a cuisine we have positive attitudes towards. At the time of decision, it doesn't matter whether a Chinese restaurant in Poland actually serves Chinese food.

At the same time, however, the attitudes that individuals have formed will guide their exploration. In other words, they will be more likely to choose to approach and engage with objects or persons to which they have formed more positive attitudes. Hence, the relationship between experience and attitude formation is essentially dynamic: attitudes are formed on the basis of feedback experiences, while at the same time such feedback experiences depend on behaviours that are guided by attitudes (Eiser et al., 2008). As a result for many of us positive experiences will tend to predominate over negative ones. If we believe that an object is bad and unattractive, we will try to avoid it, but in doing so we will limit the information about the object's true valence, and hence fail to learn whether their initial negative evaluations were correct or incorrect. Thus, our newly formed attitudes may be biased (Fazio et al., 2004; Fazio et al., 2015).

Attitude development as a function of exploratory behaviour contains a certain irony. The results of experiments conducted by Fazio et al. (2004) illuminated two valence asymmetries: one in learning and one in generalisation. The learning asymmetry indicates that positive objects are more likely to be mistaken as negative than negative objects are to be mistaken as positive. However, given that generalisation occurs as a function of the values one has come to associate with the various stimuli that have been presented, this learning asymmetry produces a tendency for novel stimuli to be classified as negative instead of positive, because it is "safer" that way. And this, in turn, leads people to believe that their world consists of more negative than positive objects.

One strategy for reducing risk is to avoid objects of uncertain valence (like never trying a new food), but this also reduces the possibility of novel rewards. In real life, however, we can reduce the risk of exploration through accepting advice from others. If we are planning a dinner, a restaurant guide book or the opinion of our friends could be useful.

3.8 Self-Perception

In the **self-perception** theory, Bem (1968, 1972) assumes that people, in part, "know" their own attitudes, emotions, and other internal states by inferring them from observing their own behaviours and/or the circumstances in which these behaviours occur. Thus, if internal cues are weak, ambiguous, or uninterpretable, the person is in the same functional position as an external observer who must necessarily rely on the same external cues to infer the performer's internal states.

From this perspective, an attitude is an individual's self-description of her affinities for and aversions to some identifiable aspect of her environment (Bem, 1968). Each of us observes our affect in relation to others, our cognitions, our smoking, eating habits, sexual arousal, or fighting. Bem (1972) assumes that explanations of own reactions, decisions, and

> **Self-perception**. People, in part, infer their own attitudes, emotions, and other internal states by observing their own behaviours and/or the circumstances in which these behaviours occur.

choices are generally located in the external world (someone provoked us, someone offered a large reward, someone did a favour for us previously, etc.). However, when we cannot identify such factors or when they seem unlikely to us as explanations for our own reactions, we come to the conclusion that the root causes lie within – in our own attitudes and inclinations. Therefore, operationally, it is our descriptions of those observations that comprise our attitudes, and our belief and attitude statements are viewed as "inferences" from her observations. An individual's belief and attitude expressions and the beliefs and attitudes that an outside observer would attribute to her are often functionally equivalent. In both cases, these are "inferences" from the same evidence: the overt the individual's behaviour. Therefore, the mechanism of inference about our own attitudes is analogous to that which underlies our inference about the attitudes of other people. Using the example given by Dolinski (2016, p. 12), if you ask a man whether his wife likes soap operas, he might respond, "I think so, after all, she does watch them all the time." But what if we pose the same question to the wife? If she said, "I think I do, after all, I watch them every day," then it could be said her process of deduction about her own TV preferences is exactly the same as her husband's. The woman in this example might first wonder if she watches soap operas because she feels lonely and thus has "company," or perhaps to have something to talk about with her friends. If it turns out that this review of the circumstances fails to indicate any external factors influencing her choice to watch soap operas, she will then search for the answers within herself. She thus comes to the conclusion that she likes this form of entertainment.

According to Bem (1968), it would appear that individuals learn to describe objects in their environment through some process of discrimination training. Further, it would appear that such descriptions can and do generalise along several dimensions to similar stimuli with which an individual has had no direct previous encounter. Attitudes, as self-descriptions, can become "internalised" variants of the attitudinal descriptions used, for example, by parents to instruct or control the behaviour of their children. Thus, attitudes can serve as self-instructions in the way that interpersonal instructions do.

It should be strongly emphasised that Bem (1972) does not claim that thinking about the causes of one's own behaviours is the sole source of knowledge about self. Sometimes, however, we have no other foundations for coming to conclusions about our own preferences and attitudes.

3.9 Beliefs as Source of Attitudes

Conscious beliefs about an object's attributes may also form the basis for attitude formation. **Beliefs** refer to the information people have about themselves and their social and physical environment. They offer answers to questions about what we take to be true and how we know.

Beliefs. The information people have about themselves and their social and physical environments which they take on to be true.

Expectancy-value model. This model assumes that individuals combine their beliefs about an object's attributes with the values they place on those attributes to form an attitude.

From this perspective, our beliefs are what precede and direct the formation of an overall positive or negative evaluation of the object. That is, people presumably acquire information about an object and deduce their attitudes from that information, even if they do so with only minimal conscious attention. Viewing attitude as resulting from beliefs also assumes that our emotional attitude towards an object is the effect of conscious reflection on its strengths and weaknesses. In other words, the attitude is rational.

These assumptions form the basis of Fishbein and Ajzen's (1975) **expectancy-value model of attitude** and their theory of reasoned action (see Section 4.3.1). The expectancy-value model suggests that individuals combine their beliefs about an object's attributes with the values they place on those attributes to form an attitude. A belief is the attribution of any property to an attitude object (e.g., "A good grade on the final exam increases my chances of getting a good job") as a result of observation, inference, or receiving information from some source. Such a property can be attributed with varying strength, meaning that people may differ in their estimates of whether a given object possesses this property (some believe that a good grade accurately reflects competence, while others do not). Furthermore, each belief also involves a partial evaluation of the object, depending on the valence of this attribute (some may believe that good grades signal a lack of social competence). Ultimately, the overall attitude towards the object is the sum of the products of the strengths of all beliefs and the partial evaluations implied by these beliefs.

For example, van der Plight and de Vries (1998) asked the participants to indicate their attitude towards smoking and their smoking behaviour. Attitudes were assessed by a direct attitude measure (the semantic differential) and a series of 15 belief statements about the possible consequences of smoking. Next, respondents were asked to select the three consequences they found most important. The attitude score based on the three most important beliefs and that based on all beliefs were strongly and similarly correlated with the direct attitude score ($r = .63$ and $r = .64$, respectively). In contrast, the attitude score based on the remaining (less important) 12 beliefs correlated with the direct attitude score significantly but weakly (r = .15).

The results of this study, as well as many others, suggest that although beliefs about the object are an important factor influencing attitude, they are not the only factor.

Further Reading

Banaji, M. R., & Heiphetz, L. (2010). Attitudes. In S. T. Fiske, D. T. Gilbert, & G. Lindzey (Eds.), *Handbook of social psychology* (Vol. 1, 5th ed., pp. 353–393). Hoboken, NJ: John Wiley & Sons.

References

Banaji, M. R., & Heiphetz, L. (2010). Attitudes. In S. T. Fiske, D. T. Gilbert, & G. Lindzey (Eds.), *Handbook of social psychology* (Vol. 1, 5th ed., pp. 353–393). Hoboken, NJ: John Wiley & Sons.

Bandura, A. (1965). Vicarious processes: A case of no-trial learning. In L. Berkowitz (Ed.), *Advances in social experimental psychology* (Vol. 2, pp. 1–55). New York: Academic Press.

Bell, E., Kandler, C., & Riemann, R. (2018). Genetic and environmental influences on sociopolitical attitudes: Addressing some gaps in the new paradigm. *Politics and the Life Sciences, 37*(2), 236–249.

Bem, D. J. (1968). Attitudes as self-descriptions: Another look at the attitude-behavior link. In A. G. Greenwald, T. C. Brock, & T. M. Ostrom (Eds.), *Psychological foundations of attitudes* (pp. 197–215). New York: Academic Press.

Bem, D. J. (1972). Self-perception theory. In L. Berkowitz (Ed.), *Advances in experimental social psychology* (Vol. 6, pp. 1–62). New York: Academic Press.

Bornstein, R. F. (1989). Exposure and affect: Overview and meta-analysis of research, 1968–1987. *Psychological Bulletin, 106*(2), 265–289.

Cacioppo, J. T., Marshall-Goodell, B. S., Tassinary, L. G., & Petty, R. E. (1992). Rudimentary determinants of attitudes: Classical conditioning is more effective when prior knowledge about the attitude stimulus is low than high. *Journal of Experimental Social Psychology, 28*(3), 207–233.

Chabris, C. F., Lee, J. J., Cesarini, D., Benjamin, D. J., & Laibson, D. I. (2015). The fourth law of behavior genetics. *Current Directions in Psychological Science, 24*(4), 304–312.

Charney, E., & English, W. (2012). Candidate genes and political behavior. *American Political Science Review, 106*(1), 1–34.

Coates, J. M., & Herbert, J. (2008). Endogenous steroids and financial risk taking on a London trading floor. *Proceedings of the National Academy of Sciences of the United States of America, 105*(16), 6167–6172.

De Houwer, J. (2007). A conceptual and theoretical analysis of evaluative conditioning. *Spanish Journal of Psychology, 10*(2), 230–241.

deCharms, R., & Rosenbaum, M. E. (1960). The problem of vicarious experience. In D. Willner (Ed.), *Decisions, values and groups* (pp. 267–277). Oxford: Pergamon Press.

Deutsch, M., & Gerard, H. B. (1955). A study of normative and informational social influences upon individual judgment. *Journal of Abnormal and Social Psychology, 51*(3), 629–636.

Dolinski, D. (2016). *Techniques of social influence: The psychology of gaining compliance.* Hove: Routledge.

Durante, K. M., Rae, A., & Griskevicius, V. (2013). The fluctuating female vote: Politics, religion, and the ovulatory cycle. *Psychological Science, 24*(6), 1007–1016.

Eiser, J. R. (2004). Putting Humpty together again: Attitude organization from a connectionist perspective. In G. Haddock, & G. R. Maio (Eds.), *Contemporary perspectives on the psychology of attitudes* (pp. 325–343). New York: Psychology Press.

Eiser, J. R., Stafford, T., & Fazio, R. H. (2008). Expectancy confirmation in attitude learning: A connectionist account. *European Journal of Social Psychology, 38*(6), 1023–1032.

Fausto-Sterling, A. (1997). Beyond difference: A biologist's perspective. *Journal of Social Issues, 53*(2), 233–258.

Fazio, R. H., Eiser, J. R., Shook, N. J. (2004). Attitude formation through exploration: Valence asymmetries. *Journal of Personality and Social Psychology, 87*(3), 293–311.

Fazio, R. H., Lenn, T. M., & Effrein, E. A. (1983–1984). Spontaneous attitude formation. *Social Cognition, 2*(1), 217–234.

Fazio, R. H., Pietri, E. S., Rocklage, M. D., & Shook, N. J. (2015). Positive versus negative valence: Asymmetries in attitude formation and generalization as fundamental individual differences. In J. M. Olson, & M. P. Zanna (Eds.), *Advances in experimental social psychology* (Vol. 51, pp. 97–146). Burlington: Academic Press.

Fishbein, M., & Ajzen, I. (1975). *Belief, attitude, intention and behavior: An introduction to theory and research.* Reading, MA: Addison-Wesley.

Gidengil, E., O'Neill, B., & Young, L. (2010). Her mother's daughter? The influence of childhood socialization on women's political engagement. *Journal of Women, Politics & Policy, 31*(4), 334–355.

Halbeisen, G., Walther, E., & Schneider, M. (2017). Evaluative conditioning and the development of attitudes in early childhood. *Child Development, 88*(5), 1536–1543.

Hildum, D. C., & Brown, R. W. (1956). Verbal reinforcement and interviewer bias. *Journal of Abnormal and Social Psychology, 53*(1), 108–111.

Hilmert, C. J., Kulik, J. A., & Christenfeld, N. J. S. (2006). Positive and negative opinion modeling: The influence of another's similarity and dissimilarity. *Journal of Personality and Social Psychology, 90*(3), 440–452.

Hofmann, W., De Houwer, J., Peruguni, M., Baeyens, F., & Crombez, G. (2010). Evaluative conditioning in humans: A meta-analysis. *Psychological Bulletin, 136*(3), 390–421.

Insko, C. A. (1965). Verbal reinforcement of attitude. *Journal of Personality and Social Psychology, 2*(4), 621–623.

Iyengar, S. (1976). Childhood learning of partisanship in a new nation: The case of Andhra Pradesh. *American Journal of Political Science, 20*(3), 407–423.

Kanekar, S. (1976). Observational learning of attitudes: A behavioral analysis. *European Journal of Social Psychology, 6*(1), 5–24.

Krosnick, J. A., Betz, A. L., Jussim, L. J., & Lynn, A. R. (1992). Subliminal conditioning of attitudes. *Personality and Social Psychology Bulletin, 18*(2), 152–162.

Lee, A. Y. (2001). The mere exposure effect: An uncertainty reduction explanation revisited. *Personality and Social Psychology Bulletin, 27*(10), 1255–1266.

Newcomb, T. M. (1952). Attitude development as a function of reference group. In G. E. Swanson, T. M. Newcomb, & E. L. Hartley (Eds.), *Readings in social psychology* (pp. 420–430). New York: Holt.

Olson, J. M., Vernon, P. A., Harris, J. A., & Jang, K. (2001). The heritability of attitudes: A study of twins. *Journal of Personality and Social Psychology, 80*(6), 845–860.

Rescorla, R. A. (1988). Pavlovian conditioning: It's not what you think it is. *American Psychologist, 43*(3), 151–160.

Skinner, B. F. (1953). *Science and human behavior.* New York: The Macmillan Company.

Skinner, A. L., & Perry, S. (2019). Are attitudes contagious? Exposure to biased nonverbal signals can create novel social attitudes. *Personality and Social Psychology Bulletin, 46*(4), 514–524.

Staats, A. W., & Staats, C. K. (1958). Attitudes established by classical conditioning. *Journal of Abnormal and Social Psychology, 57*(1), 37–40.

Staats, C. K., Staats, A. W., & Heard, W. G. (1980). Attitude development and ratio of reinforcement. *Sociometry, 23*(4), 338–350.

Tesser, A. (1993). The importance of heritability in psychological research: The case of attitudes. *Psychological Review, 100*(1), 129–142.

van der Pligt, J., & de Vries, N. K. (1998). Belief importance in expectancy-value models of attitudes. *Journal of Applied Social Psychology, 28*(15), 1339–1354.

Van Ditmars, M. M. (2023). Political socialization, political gender gaps and the intergenerational transmission of left-right ideology. *European Journal of Political Research, 62*(1), 3–24.

Walther, E., Nagengast, B., & Trasselli, C. (2005). Evaluative conditioning in social psychology: Facts and speculations. *Cognition and Emotion, 19*(2), 175–196.

Zajonc, R. B. (1968). Attitudinal effects of mere exposure. *Journal of Personality and Social Psychology, 9*(2, Pt. 2), 1–27.

Zajonc, R. B. (1980). Feeling and thinking: Preferences need no inferences. *American Psychologist, 35*(2), 151–175.

Chapter 4

Consequences of Attitudes

Information Processing and Behaviour

Attitude theory is valuable only if having a specific attitude has any impact on our functioning. The questioning by some researchers, especially in the 1960s (e.g., Wicker, 1969), of the usefulness of the attitude construct in psychology and other disciplines led to the initiation of numerous research programmes. Their goal was to test and demonstrate whether attitudes influence how and what information we seek, how we process or elaborate on it, and, most importantly, what the relationship is between attitudes and behaviour. The results of these studies consistently provide new evidence leading to a clear conclusion: attitudes significantly influence our thoughts, simple and quick reactions, and more complex actions.

4.1 The Impact of Attitudes on Attention and Memory

One of the most important starting points for analysing the impact of attitudes on information processing was the observation that people strive to have consistent beliefs about a given issue or object and that they strive to act consistently, in accordance with them. This assumption, or **principle of cognitive congruence**, is the essence of the theory of **cognitive dissonance** developed by Festinger (1957). In numerous studies, he found that when new information (from outside or as a result of our own thinking) contradicts our attitudes, or we behave in a way that is inconsistent with them, an unpleasant emotional state (dissonance) arises within us. We can eliminate this in several ways. Based on the new information, we can change our attitudes, beliefs, and behaviours or find justifications for our behaviour that contradicts our attitudes. Another way to avoid

> **Cognitive dissonance**. An unpleasant emotional state that arises when an individual holds conflicting beliefs, values, or behaviours regarding the same object.

DOI: 10.4324/9781003589174-5

dissonance is to seek out or notice information that is consistent with our attitudes and avoid or challenge the value of information that is inconsistent with our attitudes. In other words, we are motivated to view the world through the prism of our attitudes to defend ourselves against (real or imagined) threats to our beliefs or worldview. This mode of functioning is referred to in contemporary psychology as **motivated social cognition**. It refers to the fact that "people rely on cognitive processes and representations to arrive at their desired conclusion, but motivation plays a role in determining which of these will be used on a given occasion" (Kunda, 1990, p. 480). The opposite of such **defensive motivation** is motivation to be accurate or **accuracy motivation**. However, the latter generally requires more effort and appears to occur less automatically.

> **Motivated social cognition**. People rely on cognitive processes and representations to arrive at their desired conclusion, but motivation plays a role in determining which of these will be used on a given occasion.
>
> **Accuracy motivation.** Desire to develop valid attitudes based on facts.
>
> **Defence motivation.** Desire to form or defend a specific attitude.
>
> **Selective exposure**. It involves seeking information that is consistent with one's current attitudes and disregarding or avoiding information that contradicts them.

One manifestation of motivational social cognition related to attitudes is the **selective exposure effect** (e.g., Frey, 1986). Selective exposure refers to seeking information that is consistent with one's current attitudes and disregarding or avoiding information that contradicts them. This type of selectivity is referred to as a **congeniality bias** (e.g., Eagly & Chaiken, 1993). This strategy is particularly pronounced and frequently studied in relation to political attitudes (e.g., Leeper & Slothuus, 2014). For example, supporters of a given political party, if they believe a given media outlet (e.g., a television station or online news portal) is biased and hostile, will obtain information from other sources that confirm their support for the party. Selective exposure is therefore also one of the factors that "locks" people into filter bubbles or **echo chambers** (see Section 12.3). In a meta-analysis of selective exposure studies, Hart et al. (2009) confirmed that there was a significantly stronger preference for seeking congenial over uncongenial information, but the magnitude of this effect was moderate. Furthermore, congeniality bias depended on, or was moderated by, a number of factors. For example, it was stronger when individuals were more confident in their attitudes and beliefs and weaker when participants were additionally entrenched in their views before information selection.

In addition to their motivational impact on attention, attitudes can also influence it automatically. They can therefore serve an **orientation function**. For example, Roskos-Ewoldsen and Fazio (1992) observed that the probability of noticing an object strongly associated with an attitude was significantly higher than one that was weakly associated with it or was "novel." This may translate into the fact that, for example, when a job interviewer strongly associates a person's ethnicity with their attitudes (positive or negative), a candidate's skin colour may be noticed more quickly and elicit stronger affective reactions than the candidate's gender or professional experience. As a result, judgements about the candidate will be biased based on the attribute of the object that was noticed more quickly.

Attitudes also influence what is remembered and retained. In this case, their influence may be selective: we remember better what is consistent with an attitude than what is inconsistent with it. This effect was confirmed in the meta-analysis conducted by Eagly et al. (1999), although its strength is modest. This is partly because there is also a counter-tendency to better remember what is inconsistent with one's attitude (e.g., to better reflect on it and counter-argue). It therefore appears that the influence of attitudes on memory primarily relies on the fact that information that is related to the attitude is remembered better than information that is not (e.g., neutral information). Whether this information is consistent with the attitude or not depends on factors such as the degree of engagement of the attitude object, that is, whether defensive or accuracy motivation is present.

4.2 The Impact of Attitudes on Information Processing

The motivation to defend one's attitudes and beliefs also influences the processing, elaboration, and interpretation of information. One manifestation of this is **biased perception**, or perceiving the same phenomenon or object differently depending on one's attitudes. An example of this process is the **hostile media**

> **Hostile media phenomenon**. It occurs when opposing partisans perceive identical news coverage of a controversial issue as biased against their own side.

Biased assimilation. This phenomenon occurs when even a random set of outcomes and events can appear to lend support for an entrenched position, and both sides in a given debate can have their position bolstered by the same set of data.

Attitude polarisation. A non-qualitative shift in attitude towards the more extreme end of the scale.

phenomenon. Vallone, Ross, and Lepper (1985) studied how "pro-Israeli" and "pro-Arab" students perceived and evaluated a television report about the killing of civilians in Palestinian refugee camps in Lebanon. Each group was presented with exactly the same coverage. The researchers found that, depending on their attitude, the position contained in the message was assessed as hostile or supportive of the other side.

Another manifestation of the influence of attitudes on information processing is **biased assimilation**. This phenomenon occurs when "even a random set of outcomes and events can appear to lend support for an entrenched position, and both sides in a given debate can have their position bolstered by the same set of data" (Lord et al., 1979, p. 2099). This effect was demonstrated in a classic study by Lord, Ross, and Lepper (1979). They asked students who were either proponents or opponents of the death penalty to read and evaluate two (actually fictional) scientific articles. One article provided support for the conclusion that the death penalty is an effective deterrent to murder, and the other article presented evidence for the opposite conclusion. The researchers found that students rated evidence consistent with their attitudes as more persuasive and probative than information that challenged their attitudes. Furthermore, they assimilated information consistent with their own attitudes. Consequently, exposure to two-sided messages did not soften initial attitudes towards the death penalty but rather strengthened them, ultimately making them more extreme. Biased assimilation resulted in **attitude polarisation**. Therefore, individuals tend to accept evidence confirming their attitudes at face value, while simultaneously judging contradictory evidence as worthless, erroneous, and biased, and subsequently rejecting it. Furthermore, biased assimilation is not necessarily a conscious process; it can also occur automatically (e.g., Ledgerwood & Chaiken, 2007).

It should be emphasised that, as with selective exposure, the consequences of biased perception and assimilation processes can include locking oneself in "one's own world," where only those who agree with one are present – in echo chambers (see Section 12.3).

The influence of attitudes on information processing can also be manifested through **motivated directional reasoning**, which manifests itself in the cognitive effort to defend one's attitudes (Kunda, 1990). This can occur especially when we receive information that is inconsistent with our attitudes towards an object. This may result in deeper processing of the information to find justification for its explanation (often through distortion or a different interpretation) or rejection. This influence of attitudes is demonstrated by Petersen et al.'s (2013) findings when controversial political proposals are attributed to the party supported by respondents.

Attitudinal heuristic. It is the use of an evaluative relationship that an individual maintains with an object as the strategy for problem-solving by assigning an object to either a favourable or an unfavourable category.

However, attitudes can also "switch off" thinking if we rely on them as heuristics. According to Pratkanis (1988, p. 258),

> an **attitudinal heuristic** is one that uses the evaluative relationship that an individual maintains with an object as the strategy for problem-solving by assigning an object to either a favourable category (for which strategies of favouring, approaching, and protecting are appropriate) or to an unfavourable category (for which strategies of disfavouring, avoiding, and harming are appropriate).

Thus, the emergence of an attitude object does not require much deliberation because it is "known" to be good (or bad). Therefore, there is no need to analyse or interpret any additional information related to it. After all, we know what to expect from a friend, an unsupported politician, or what a dish containing tofu will taste like regardless of its other ingredients.

4.3 The Influence of Attitudes on Behaviour

In response, when the existence of the relationship between attitudes and behaviour began to be questioned in the 1960s, two complementary approaches emerged: one focused on various aspects of attitude measurement, and the other focused on finding variables that might moderate, or modify, the strength of the relationship between attitudes and behaviour. The first of these approaches found expression in the theory of reasoned action (TRA; Fishbein & Ajzen, 1975) and its expanded and developed successor, the **theory of planned behaviour** (TPB; Ajzen, 1991).

4.3.1 Theory of Planned Behaviour

Theory of planned behaviour (TPB). A theory that assumes that three core components: attitude towards behaviour, subjective norms, and perceived behavioural control, together shape an individual's behavioural intentions, which are the primary determinants of that behaviour.

One reason for the weak relationship between attitude and behaviour may be the lack of correspondence between measures of these two variables (see Ajzen, 1996). Therefore, one cannot accurately predict a specific behaviour (e.g., chaining oneself to a tree to protect a nature reserve from destruction) based on a general measure of attitude (e.g., a measure of environmental attitudes). This can be achieved if, instead of measuring general attitudes towards an object, we measure attitudes towards behaviour towards it. However, stopping there may be sufficient. Although measures of general attitudes towards objects are weak predictors of single, specific behaviours, they become more useful in predicting behaviour occurring in a wider range of situations and contexts. Fishbein and Ajzen (see Ajzen, 1996) therefore proposed that multiple behaviours be assessed and that these data be aggregated to increase the predictive power of general attitude measures. Therefore, predicting an individual's behaviour based on their environmental attitude will be more accurate when we know their attitudes towards tying themselves to a tree in a nature reserve, green shopping, wild tourism, water conservation, etc.

These two principles (correspondence and aggregation) underlie the TRA (Fishbein & Ajzen, 1975) and its expanded version, the TPB (Ajzen, 1991). It should be emphasised that both theories assume that attitudes are based on beliefs of which the individual is conscious, and therefore, the process of arriving at behaviour is rational.

According to the *TRA* (Fishbein & Ajzen, 1975), the direct cause of behaviour is **behavioural intention**, or the conscious desire to perform a certain action. All other influences on behaviour occur solely through this intention. The two factors that shape intention are attitude towards a given action and subjective norm. **Attitude towards a behaviour** is defined as the sum of the products "belief × value." Each of these products represents the subjective belief or expectation that a given behaviour will result in a certain consequence, multiplied by the subjective value of that consequence. For example, a man believes that by purchasing a set of carpentry tools, he will be able to make furniture for his living room (a positive consequence, with moderate subjective probability), but he will first have to learn woodworking, which requires both time and additional financial outlay (a negative consequence, with high probability).

These two aspects combined would result in a moderately positive attitude towards purchasing tools.

The second determinant of behavioural intention is **subjective norm**. This construct is also expressed as the sum of the products of two elements. The first is the normative belief that a significant person or group believes that an individual should perform a given action, and the second is the motivation to comply with this person or group. For example, a man is convinced that his wife does not support his carpentry initiatives and would prefer to have exclusive furniture made by a professional. In this situation, the man may want to avoid conflict with his wife, which negatively affects his intention to purchase tools. However, if there are more people whose opinions he values equally or more (e.g., colleagues, brother, or daughter) and who support his idea, then his intention will be the resultant of all these opinions.

The *TPB* (Ajzen, 1991) considers, in addition to all of the above, another variable that can influence behaviour: **perceived behavioural control**. Its inclusion in the model stems from the fact that not every behaviour can be performed, even when attitudes and norms favour it. If, for example, a man lacks a budget or a workshop, his intention will not translate into behaviour. Furthermore, according to the TPB, perceived behavioural control influences behaviour either indirectly, through behavioural intention, or directly, to the extent that it accurately reflects the subject's actual control over a given behaviour.

Both of these theories have been tested in hundreds of studies in fields as diverse as health, tourism, environmental behaviour, and consumer behaviour. These studies have also been the subject of numerous meta-analyses, which have focused either on the full theory or on its individual components (e.g., Armitage & Conner, 2001; Trafimow et al., 2002). The conclusion that can be drawn from them is relatively clear: the TPB has proven to be a very good model for explaining the relationship between attitude and behaviour.

4.3.2 Moderators of the Attitude-Behaviour Relationship

The second approach to analysing the relationship between attitude and behaviour focuses on the importance of various factors that modify it, that is, moderators.

The first category is related to the characteristics of the attitude itself, primarily its **strength** (see Section 2.1). Numerous studies confirm that the stronger the attitude, the better it predicts behaviour (e.g., Howe & Krosnick, 2017; Visser et al., 2006). That is, an attitude is more closely linked to behaviour the more important, accessible, intense, extreme, certain, elaborate, affectively-cognitively consistent, and non-ambivalent it is.

Meta-cognitive processes (metacognition). People's thoughts about their own thought processes.

Self-validation. A subjective sense that one's thoughts are valid or appropriate to use.

For example, Sivacek and Crano (1982) demonstrated that the degree to which an individual perceives an attitude as hedonically relevant affects the relationship between attitudes and behaviour. This is because, according to their **vested interest** hypothesis, when the behaviours suggested by a specific attitude have clear and obvious hedonic relevance for an actor, then attitude-behaviour consistency is maximised. In one of their experiments, Sivacek and Crano (1982) found that respondents' willingness to work actively against the passage of a referendum that would raise the legal drinking age was found to be associated with their age (and consequently, the degree to which this change in law would affect them).

Meta-cognitive processes (i.e., "thoughts about thoughts"), such as self-validation, may also be a moderator of the relationship between attitude and behaviour (Briñol & Petty, 2009, 2022). The core notion of **self-validation** theory (see Section 7.1.5) is that thoughts become more consequential for judgement and action as the perceived validity of the thoughts is increased. Instead of focusing on the objective accuracy of thoughts, self-validation refers to a subjective sense that one's thoughts are valid or appropriate to use. People come to rely on any thought more when they perceive that thought is likely to be true (cognitive validation) or because they feel good about the thought (affective validation).

From a different perspective, Lord et al. (1984) believe that attitude-behaviour consistency occurs when the stimulus in the behavioural response situation matches the perceived stimulus in the verbal response situation. According to them, individuals' attitudes towards social groups are formed based on information and imagined reactions to the **prototypical group member**. When they encounter a specific group member whose characteristics match well those of the "attitude prototype," individuals display attitude-behaviour consistency; when the match is poor, they display attitude-behaviour inconsistency. Therefore, attitudes towards a social group will match behaviour towards a member of that group only to the extent that the target person matches the prototype that served as the basis for the attitude in the first place.

The list of potential moderators of the attitude-behaviour relationship is, of course, open-ended. Nevertheless, years of research on the relationship between attitude and behaviour have contributed significantly to its better understanding. Not only have they dispelled previous pessimism about the usefulness of the attitude construct, but they have also enabled the identification of important moderators of this relationship. We are now able to predict with high confidence when attitudes will be strongly related to behaviour and when they will not. Furthermore, research has illuminated the processes through which attitudes can influence behaviour.

Further Readings

Ajzen, I. (1996). *Attitudes, personality, and behavior.* Chicago, IL: Dorsey Press.

Bohner, G., & Dickel, N. (2011). Attitudes and attitude change. *Annual Review of Psychology, 62*, 391–417.

References

Ajzen, I. (1991). The theory of planned behavior. *Organizational Behavior and Human Decision Processes, 50*(2), 179–211.

Ajzen, I. (1996). *Attitudes, personality, and behavior.* Chicago, IL: Dorsey Press.

Armitage, C. J., & Conner, M. (2001). Efficacy and the theory of planned behaviour: A meta-analytic review. *British Journal of Social Psychology, 40*(4), 471–499.

Bohner, G., & Dickel, N. (2011). Attitudes and attitude change. *Annual Review of Psychology, 62*, 391–417.

Briñol, P., & Petty, R. E. (2009). Persuasion: Insights from the self-validation hypothesis. In M. P. Zanna (Ed.), *Advances in experimental social psychology* (Vol. 41, pp. 69–118). New York: Academic Press.

Briñol, P., & Petty, R. E. (2022). Self-validation theory: An integrative framework for understanding when thoughts become consequential. *Psychological Review, 129*(2), 340–367.

Eagly, A. H., & Chaiken, S. (1993). *The psychology of attitudes.* Fort Worth, TX: Harcourt Brace Jovanovich College Publishers.

Eagly, A. H., Chen, S., Chaiken, S., & Shaw-Barnes, K. (1999). The impact of attitudes on memory: An affair to remember. *Psychological Bulletin, 125*(1), 64–89.

Festinger, L. (1957). *A theory of cognitive dissonance.* Stanford, CA: Stanford University Press.

Fishbein, M., & Ajzen, I. (1975). *Belief, attitude, intention and behavior: An introduction to theory and research.* Reading, MA: Addison-Wesley.

Frey, D. (1986). Recent research on selective exposure to information. In L. Berkowitz (Ed.), *Advances in experimental social psychology* (Vol. 19, pp. 41–80). New York: Academic Press.

Hart, W., Albarracín, D., Eagly, A. H., Brechan, I., Lindberg, M. J., & Merril, L. (2009). Feeling validated versus being correct: A meta-analysis of selective exposure to information. *Psychological Bulletin, 135*(4), 555–588.

Howe, L. C., & Krosnick, J. A. (2017). Attitude strength. *Annual Review of Psychology, 68*, 327–351.

Kunda, Z. (1990). The case for motivated reasoning. *Psychological Bulletin, 108*(3), 480–498.

Ledgerwood, A., & Chaiken, S. (2007). Priming us and them: Automatic assimilation and contrast in group attitudes. *Journal of Personality and Social Psychology, 93*(6), 940–956.

Leeper, T. J., & Slothuus, R. (2014). Political parties, motivated reasoning, and public opinion formation. *Advances in Political Psychology, 39*(Supp. 1), 129–156.

Lord, C. G., Lepper, M. R., & Mackie, D. (1984). Attitude prototypes as determinants of attitude-behavior consistency. *Journal of Personality and Social Psychology, 46*(6), 1254–1266.

Lord, C. G., Ross, L., & Lepper, M. R. (1979). Biased assimilation and attitude polarization: The effects of prior theories on subsequently considered evidence. *Journal of Personality and Social Psychology, 37*(11), 2098–2109.

Petersen, M. B., Skov, M., Serritzlew, S., & Ramsøy, T. (2013). Motivated reasoning and political parties: Evidence for increased processing in the face of party cues. *Political Behavior, 35*(4), 831–854.

Pratkanis, A. R. (1988). The attitude heuristic and selective fact identification. *British Journal of Social Psychology, 27*(3), 257–263.

Roskos-Ewoldsen, D. R., & Fazio, R. H. (1992). On the orienting value of attitudes: Attitude accessibility as a determinant of an object's attraction of visual attention. *Journal of Personality and Social Psychology, 63*(2), 198–211.

Sivacek, J., & Crano, W. D. (1982). Vested interest as a moderator of attitude-behavior consistency. *Journal of Personality and Social Psychology, 43*(2), 210–221.

Trafimow, D., Sheeran, P., Conner, M., & Finlay, K. A. (2002). Evidence that perceived behavioural control is a multidimensional construct: Perceived control and perceived difficulty. *British Journal of Social Psychology, 41*(1), 101–121.

Vallone, R. P., Ross, L., & Lepper, M. R. (1985). The hostile media phenomenon: Biased perception and perceptions of media bias in coverage of the Beirut massacre. *Journal of Personality and Social Psychology, 49*(3), 577–585.

Visser, P. S., Bizer, G. Y., & Krosnick, J. A. (2006). Exploring the latent structure of strength-related attitude attributes. In M. P. Zanna (Ed.), *Advances in experimental social psychology* (Vol. 38, pp. 1–67). New York: Academic Press.

Wicker, A. W. (1969). Attitudes versus actions: The relationship of verbal and overt behavioral responses to attitude objects. *Journal of Social Issues, 25*(4), 41–78.

Chapter 5

Persuasion

Classic Studies on Attitude Change

What is **persuasion**? We define it as the use of communication to change others' attitudes (Cwalina & Koniak, 2025). Therefore, persuasion encompasses any situation in which a person or group uses communication to influence how others evaluate something. In psychology, the term "persuasion" is used interchangeably with "attitude change." However, **attitude change** is a broader concept, as it may also include non-communication-based changes in attitudes. For example, we may dislike a previously liked dessert after receiving food poisoning from it. Attitude change may also result from self-persuasion when a person persuades themselves to change their own attitude. Self-persuasion can occur without any external influence, for example, through mere thought about an object of attitude. However, it may also be a consequence of receiving the communication that initiates it.

5.1 Effects of Persuasion

Persuasion attempts may lead to different types of attitude changes. The first is when a person moves from one side of the evaluative continuum to the other (e.g., pro-choice person becomes pro-life or supporter of nuclear plant building becomes an opponent). This can be called **change in valence of attitude** or **qualitative change** (from negative to positive or from positive to negative) and is probably the most prototypical case for most people (Bechler et al., 2019). However, this type of change is also less common and difficult to obtain. Persuasion often results in less dramatic changes (or no changes at all), but these changes can be more consequential and persuasive efforts

Persuasion. The use of communication to change others' attitudes.

Qualitative attitude change. Change in valence of attitude – from negative to positive or from positive to negative.

DOI: 10.4324/9781003589174-6

directed on them more effective than those focusing on valence or qualitative change (Bechler et al., 2020). Thus, persuasion can result in **non-qualitative attitude change** or **change within valence**, that is, moving on an evaluative continuum without changing the side – a mild supporter can become a strong supporter, or a strong supporter can lower his or her support. The direction of this within-valence change (or modification) is also important. A shift in attitude towards the more extreme end of the scale (i.e., when a person's evaluation of something shifts from mildly positive to strongly positive) is called **polarisation**. **Depolarisation**, in turn, is the case when a person shifts attitude towards neutral point of the scale. Persuasion may also result in a **change in attitude strength** (e.g., attitude certainty, accessibility, ambivalence, or importance; see Section 2.1), both when the valence of the attitude changes qualitatively or non-qualitatively, and when there is no change in valence. For example, after persuasion, people may still think that a nuclear plant should be closed or that their favourite fizzy drink was better when it contained sugar instead of aspartame. However, they may be less certain that they evaluated it accurately, or they may perceive the issue as less important than before.

Non-qualitative attitude change. Change within valence – moving on an evaluative continuum without changing the side of the scale (e.g., move from strong opposition to mild opposition).

Attitude polarisation. A non-qualitative shift in attitude towards the more extreme end of the scale.

Attitude depolarisation. A non-qualitative shift in attitude towards the neutral point of the scale.

Much research on persuasion focuses only on assessing attitudes after the intervention. Since there is no initial attitude to compare, the effectiveness of persuasion in these cases is assessed by comparing the attitudes of different groups exposed to different versions of persuasive communication. For example, one group may be exposed to communication that focuses on emotion, whereas another is exposed to communication that focuses on reason. If the attitudes of one of these groups are more positive (or negative, if the goal of persuasion is to convince people that an object is bad), the type of communication presented to this group is more effective than that presented to the second group.

5.1.1 Sleeper Effect

The effectiveness of persuasive communication is usually assessed relatively soon after the message is presented and fades over time (although

> **Sleeper effect.** Delayed increase in persuasiveness of the initially noneffective message (due to initially available discounting cue becoming cognitively unavailable).

the persistence of attitude change depends on many factors, some of which will be discussed in the second part of this book). However, the reverse may be true in some situations. Immediate measurement may indicate that persuasion was unsuccessful; however, its effectiveness may increase over time. This phenomenon is known as the **sleeper effect**. This effect occurs when a discounting cue is presented alongside persuasive communication that would otherwise be effective. For example, presented arguments may be discounted and rejected if they are shown to come from an untrustworthy source or if there is a disclaimer that the information presented is false. If the recipient of such a message is persuaded by the argumentation but is made aware of such a discounting cue, he or she may show no signs of attitude change immediately after exposure. However, persuasion may increase over time as the discounting cue becomes cognitively unavailable or "dissociated" from the message in memory (Kumkale & Albarracín, 2004).

5.2 Classic Psychological Studies of Persuasion

Thinking about persuasion as a specific case of communication can help distinguish the elements of this communication that determine its effectiveness. One of the first empirical programmes concerned the factors affecting change in attitude stemmed from experiences related to propaganda campaigns during the Second World War. These studies were conducted at Yale University and published in the book *Communication and Persuasion* (Hovland et al., 1953). This line of research assumes that when processing persuasive communication, people not only evoke pre-existing habitual opinions and attitudes but also learn new ones as suggested by the persuasive message itself. Therefore, successive persuasion should stimulate an individual to think about not only the initial opinion but also the new one that is recommended in the communication. It should also lead to overcoming the old habitual opinions of the newly learned ones (which should result in a change in attitude). From the perspective of Yale communication studies, incentives that involve individuals' anticipations of rewards or punishments resulting from acceptance or rejection of the recommended opinion could enhance the acceptance of this new opinion. For example, communicator expertise may be an incentive. When people find that holding accurate views is rewarding, their motivation to accept expert opinions should be greater than that to accept opinions from non-experts.

Reception. One of the stages of processing persuasive communication, incorporating attention and comprehension.

Yielding. One of the stages of processing persuasive communication, that is, agreement or acceptance of the argumentation.

Persuasion variables. Elements from which persuasive communication can be constructed, such as the source, the message, the channel, the receiver, the context, or the object, and characteristics of these elements.

Yale studies also indicated that, in order to understand how persuasive communication shapes opinions and attitudes, it is necessary to recognise that each element of the communication affects the **processing stages**, such as attention, comprehension, and acceptance of the conclusion. William McGuire (1968, 2013) developed this perspective. In his model, the effectiveness of persuasive communication depends on a person progressing through several stages (**outputs**): presentation (exposure to the communication), attention, comprehension, yielding, retention (storage of the new position in memory), and behaviour (action in line with the new position). Some versions of this model include more outputs, while others focus only on two: **reception** (including attention and comprehension) and **yielding** (agreement or acceptance). Regardless of how many outputs the given version of the model distinguishes, if some of the earlier stages are unsuccessful, the persuasion process will also fail. Yielding to persuasive communication is impossible without successful reception. Therefore, the probability of a given stage occurring depends on the joint probability of all preceding stages. The **input** side of the communication process comprises the **persuasion variables** that we will describe in the next section. These are the elements from which persuasive communication can be constructed, such as the source, the message, the channel, and the characteristics of the receiver. One of McGuire's key postulates is that certain inputs (variables) can have contrasting effects on different outputs (stages). An example of such a variable is the intelligence of the receiver. The higher the intelligence, the better the reception. However, more intelligent people are less willing to yield. Consequently, the most effective persuasion occurs with recipients of moderate intelligence (McGuire, 1972).

5.3 Variables in Persuasion

This line of research also focused on identifying and testing the elements of persuasive communication that influence its effectiveness. These elements or characteristics can vary from case to case, and can be deliberately designed and selected. Further studies, conducted from different theoretical perspectives, have expanded upon the catalogue of variables proposed by Hovland, Janis, and Kelly (1953). Overall, persuasive effectiveness relates to the four components of communication indicated in Lasswell's (1948) formula: "Who," "Says What," "In What Channel," "To Whom," and "Under What Circumstances." The final component of Lasswell's formula, "With What Effect," is in fact a question about persuasive effectiveness. While the persuasive effectiveness of some variables may seem obvious based on common sense, the outcome can sometimes differ from what is expected, leading to paradoxical results. Therefore, it is crucial to understand which variables are consequential and the role each one plays in persuasive communication. Providing a complete catalogue and discussion of the characteristics of each variable and how they work would exceed the scope of this book. Instead, we will briefly highlight some of the characteristics of each variable that should be considered, as well as present the effects of some of them. Chapter 7 will also discuss the roles that variables can play in persuasion (see Briñol & Petty, 2009; Petty & Wegener, 1998).

Remember that the persuasive consequences of a given element depend on how it is perceived by the recipient and the state it induces. Furthermore, the persuasiveness of a variable depends on the characteristics of other variables, and no single element of the persuasion process should be considered universally persuasive. Persuasion is the result of many factors coming together. The same characteristic of one variable can be persuasively effective when combined with a particular characteristic of another variable. However, when combined with a different characteristic, its persuasiveness may decrease or even become counterproductive. For instance, statistical data may be persuasive when presented by an expert, yet relatively unpersuasive when presented by a layperson (Artz & Tybout, 1999).

5.3.1 Source

The first group of variables ("who") relates to the observable or suggested characteristics of the **communicator** – that is, the person or group delivering the persuasive communication. This communicator may also be referred to as the **source**, **sender**, **persuader,** or **agent**. One such characteristic is **credibility**. This is

Source (also communicator, sender, persuader, presenter, or agent). The person or group delivering the persuasive communication.

determined by the source's **expertise** (i.e., whether they are perceived as knowledgeable in a given area) and/or **trustworthiness** (i.e., whether they are perceived as honest and willing to share all the information they have on the subject). Perceived **objectivity**, or the extent to which the source is seen as biased, can also be added to this. Some people may be seen as trustworthy and honest, yet unable to see the merits of an issue objectively (Wallace et al., 2020). Another characteristic of the source relates to **attractiveness** in terms of physical and social factors (**likability**). Common sense would suggest that the better the source is evaluated on these dimensions, the higher its persuasive effectiveness. However, this is not always true. For example, based on such lay theories, one might expect that, to compensate for the weaknesses in the argument, it should be presented by an expert. However, this is actually the worst solution, since weak arguments presented by an expert are less persuasive than the same arguments presented by a layperson (Bohner et al., 2002; see Section 7.2.4).

The **non-verbal behaviour** of the speaker is a specific group of variables that can also influence the effectiveness of persuasion. For example, the acoustic properties of speech, such as pitch and volume, can affect persuasion by influencing how confident the speaker seems. Speakers who speak loudly and vary their volume are perceived as strongly endorsing their stance, which facilitates persuasion (Van Zant & Berger, 2020). However, the relationship between **speech speed** and persuasion is curvilinear: while faster speech initially increases the speaker's perceived confidence and enhances message processing, this effect eventually diminishes and can even reverse (Guyer et al., 2025). Contrary to popular belief, making more **eye contact** does not make a speaker more persuasive. In fact, it makes people more resistant to persuasion and reduces attitude change (Chen et al., 2013). Other examples of non-verbal behaviour that can influence persuasion include facial expressions, gestures, and posture. However, the manner in which they exert their influence is not always obvious and may depend on factors such as the recipient or the situation (see Section 12.1.2 for an example).

5.3.2 Message

The second group comprises variables related to the persuasive **message** ("says what"). This message deals with a persuasive **topic** or **object**, and its **importance**, primarily in relation to its **relevance** to the recipient, is the most widely studied characteristic (Petty & Cacioppo, 1990; see also Chapter 7). Messages usually contain an explicitly stated or subtly suggested **position** – they take a pro or con stance on something and portray the object in a positive or negative light. This position (as well as the arguments presented in the message) may or may not align with the receiver's attitudes (see Section 8.2). The effectiveness of persuasion depends on various characteristics related to the content, organisation, or style of the message. The **quality or strength of arguments** is a variable that is frequently manipulated in persuasion studies to test assumptions relating to dual-process persuasion models (see Chapter 7). In such studies, argument quality is typically evaluated empirically by gauging its perceived impact on members of a specific group in a particular situation. The consistency of an argument with the receiver's pre-existing attitude, and the match between the argument type and a personal characteristic of the receiver, also play a role here (see Section 12.1).

Another variable related to the message is the **quantity of arguments** presented. While increasing the number of arguments can sometimes be beneficial, particularly when people are unable or unwilling to process information (see Chapter 7), it can backfire if the arguments are weak. This emphasises the importance of understanding the entire persuasion process and the mechanisms behind it. When acting as the source or presenter, people often provide too many arguments, which decreases the persuasiveness of the message by diluting a few strong arguments with weaker ones. However, when these same individuals receive a message, they are more likely to agree with one containing fewer, stronger arguments (the **presenter's paradox**; Weaver et al., 2012). Furthermore, an increasing number of arguments can lead to suspicion and counterargumentation (Shu & Carlson, 2014).

One-sided messages present only one side of the issue, that is, arguments that support the advocated position. **Two-sided messages** also mention the other side of the issue, concluding or suggesting which position should be supported. The effectiveness of two-sided messages depends on various factors, including the amount and importance of negative information and where it is placed (see Eisend, 2006, for a review). Mentioning the negative attributes of an object may increase the effectiveness of a message when these attributes are associated with positive ones (e.g., ice cream that is rich and creamy but high in calories; Pechmann, 1992). Two-sided messages may also increase

Message. Communication intended to change recipients' attitudes, usually contains arguments and indicates or suggests the desired position.

Presenter's paradox. Presenters' failure to anticipate how receivers process information leads to the design of counterproductive messages. For example, presenters may put forward too many arguments, regardless of their quality, because they adhere to the "more is better" principle.

the receiver's attitude certainty (Rucker et al., 2008).

The stylistic and rhetorical aspects of a message can influence its persuasiveness. When presenting arguments for or against a persuasive object, the message may draw an explicit conclusion by stating whether something is good or bad, or whether it should be chosen or rejected. Alternatively, the conclusion may be left implicit and inferred by the recipient. The effectiveness of **messages without an explicit conclusion** depends on whether the recipient is motivated and able to draw their own conclusion. In this case, messages with and without conclusions may result in a similarly positive (or negative, depending on the goal) attitude. However, if this attitude is based on a conclusion inferred by the recipient, it may be stronger, that is, more accessible, than one based on an explicitly presented conclusion (Kardes, 1988). Recipients can be encouraged to draw such conclusions through **rhetorical questions**, which can increase the persuasiveness of a message, enhance processing of the message and facilitate the formation of stronger attitudes. However, rhetorical questions can sometimes be distracting (Blankenship & Craig, 2006).

> **Two-sided messages**. A message containing both positive and negative information about an object, both pro and con arguments, but more or less explicitly favouring one side of the issue, or indicating whether the object is good or bad.
>
> **Messages without an explicit conclusion (with omitted conclusion)**. A message whose position is not explicitly stated but which can be inferred from the structure of the argument.

The way in which the message is presented graphically may also be important. For example, **empty space** around a text message may reduce its persuasiveness, and conversational inferences about why it is presented this way are important here. Nevertheless, the persuasive effect of empty space can be reversed when a message contradicts the recipient's attitudes, depending on their cognitive load (Kwan et al., 2017).

5.3.3 *Channel*

The next class of variables relates to the channel or modality through which the message is conveyed ("in what channel"). Assuming the argumentation used is flawless, the **written** form is more persuasive than **audio** or **video** forms when the message is difficult to understand. This is because receivers can process written messages at their own pace, which leads to greater comprehension. However, modality does not affect comprehension for easily understood messages. Nevertheless, modality affects the yielding, with easy video messages being the most persuasive, followed by audio messages and then written messages (Chaiken & Eagly, 1976). Furthermore, video and audio messages enhance the salience of information relating to the communicator, including information unrelated to voice or physical attractiveness. For this reason, source characteristics have a greater impact on persuasion when messages are presented in video or audio form than in written form (Chaiken & Eagly, 1983). The **device** used to deliver the message may also be consequential. For instance, computers increase reliance on utilitarian information about the object of persuasion and the knowledge function of attitude compared to print media (Schlosser, 2003).

Receiver (also recipient, persuadee, or target). The person to whom the persuasive message is addressed.

5.3.4 Receiver

The **receiver**, also known as the **recipient, persuadee, or target**, is the person to whom the persuasive message is addressed. This person's **demographic characteristics**, such as gender and age, can therefore influence the effectiveness of the persuasion. For instance, activating the female gender role can result in greater susceptibility to persuasion and more superficial processing of the message (Eaton et al., 2017). This is probably due to socialisation or culture-based self-stereotyping processes. In terms of age, susceptibility to attitude change is highest in early adulthood, lowest in middle adulthood, and then increases again in later life (Visser & Krosnick, 1998). Other variables relating to the effectiveness of persuasion include the properties of the **receiver's initial attitude** (e.g., certainty or accessibility; see Section 2.1), their intelligence and **personality traits** such as the need for cognition (see Section 7.1) and self-monitoring (see Section 12.1.1). These characteristics may not be stable personality traits but can be induced situationally, as with emotions or **mood**. In most cases, a happy mood leads to less scrutiny of the message than a neutral or sad mood. However, when the message is uplifting, people in a positive mood scrutinise it more than those in a negative mood (Wegener et al., 1995).

5.3.5 Context

Situational or contextual variables ("under what circumstances") relate to a broad class of characteristics of the setting in which the persuasive communication is presented. Some of these variables affect the effectiveness of persuasion mostly due to the needs or states they induce in the receiver, or the thoughts they make available. For instance, the geometric shape of a **seating arrangement** can influence the persuasiveness of a message. Circular seating activates the need to belong, whereas angular seating activates the need to be unique. Consequently, people are more persuaded by family-oriented cues or majority support in a circular arrangement, and by self-oriented cues or minority support in an angular one (Zhu & Argo, 2013). Another example is **films**, which can induce different emotional or motivational states that affect the effectiveness of advertising during commercial breaks. Adverts based on social proof ("most popular," i.e.) may be effective during a fear-inducing film but may be counterproductive during a romantic one. The reverse is true for ads based on scarcity ("limited edition"; Griskevicius et al., 2009). Contextual variables can also include, for example, a **forewarning** of the persuasive intent or content of the message (its topic and position), which can result in resistance being induced (Wood & Quinn, 2003; see Chapter 8).

5.3.6 *Object*

The effectiveness of persuasion may also depend on variables related to the object of persuasion. These variables may be characteristics of either the recipient (e.g., how important they consider the object to be) or the message (i.e., how the object is presented). Other variables include the functions served by attitudes towards the object in question. While these functions are more closely related to the object itself, they also vary from person to person (see Section 12.1). The **psychological distance** (temporal, spatial, social, etc.) between the object of the attitude and the receiver can affect how the object is constructed or represented mentally. Consequently, arguments emphasising primary or desirability features, or general classes, are more persuasive for distant objects than arguments emphasising secondary or feasibility features, or specific cases (Fujita et al., 2008). The way in which the object is **framed** also plays a role here. When asked about prohibiting something (e.g., GMOs), people process arguments in a less biased manner, and their attitudes are more susceptible to change (i.e., depolarisation) than when they are asked about allowing the same thing (Koniak & Cwalina, 2022).

5.4 Cognitive Dissonance and Attitude Change

Attitude change may result from what others say to us or what we do. According to cognitive dissonance theory (Festinger, 1957), people

Cognitive dissonance. An unpleasant emotional state that arises when an individual holds conflicting beliefs, values, or behaviours regarding the same object.

experience discomfort, or **dissonance**, when they hold conflicting beliefs. As this is an unpleasant state, people are motivated to reduce it. This can be achieved by removing the conflicting cognitions or reducing their importance (see Harmon-Jones & Mills, 2019, for other ways of reducing dissonance). For example, a smoker who believes that smoking is harmful to health can reduce the dissonance between these two cognitions ("smoking is bad for health" and "I'm still smoking") by quitting, or by denying that smoking has harmful health consequences. The elements' resistance to change determines which ones will change as a result of dissonance.

In research, one of these dissonant cognitions is often related to an individual's behaviour. For instance, in the **induced or forced compliance paradigm**, participants are instructed to perform an action or make a statement that contradicts their beliefs or attitudes. In an experiment by Festinger and Carlsmith (1959), participants performed a boring task. They were then asked to tell the next person that the task was enjoyable. They were also paid for doing so. Half of them received \$1, and the other half received \$20. Finally, they were asked to evaluate the task. Those who received \$1 for saying the task was enjoyable rated it as more enjoyable than those who received \$20. All participants experienced cognitive dissonance: they knew the task was boring, yet they had said it was enjoyable. Therefore, they did something that went against their attitude. Those who received \$20 found it easy to reduce the dissonance by telling themselves, "I did this for \$20." However, those who received \$1 could not accept that they had done it for such a small amount of money, as this would evoke another unpleasant feeling. They also couldn't deny what they had said. In order to reduce the dissonance, they had to change their perception of the task ("I said this because I think so").

Similarly, when people choose one of two similar options (e.g., one of two equally attractive products), they begin to value the chosen option more highly in order to reduce the dissonance resulting from rejecting the other option. Likewise, when they achieve a goal after making an unpleasant effort, they value the goal more highly. This is evident in the initiation rituals required to become part of a group. Even when the group turns out to be boring and unattractive, people who underwent unpleasant activities to become members seek to justify their efforts and humiliation. One way to do this is to convince themselves that the group was worth it (see Harmon-Jones & Mills, 2019, for a review of other ways of inducing dissonance).

Further Reading

Petty, R. E., & Wegener, D. T. (1998). Attitude change: Multiple roles for persuasion variables. In D. T. Gilbert, S. T. Fiske, & G. Lindzey (Eds.), *The handbook of social psychology* (4th ed., pp. 323–390). New York: McGraw-Hill.

References

Artz, N., & Tybout, A. M. (1999). The moderating impact of quantitative information on the relationship between source credibility and persuasion: A persuasion knowledge model interpretation. *Marketing Letters, 10*, 51–63.

Bechler, C. J., Tormala, Z. L., & Rucker, D. D. (2019). Perceiving attitude change: How qualitative shifts augment change perception. *Journal of Experimental Social Psychology, 82,* 160–175.

Bechler, C. J., Tormala, Z. L., & Rucker, D. D. (2020). Choosing persuasion targets: How expectations of qualitative change increase advocacy intentions. *Journal of Experimental Social Psychology, 86,* 103911.

Blankenship, K. L., & Craig, T. Y. (2006). Rhetorical question use and resistance to persuasion: An attitude strength analysis. *Journal of Language and Social Psychology, 25*(2), 111–128.

Bohner, G., Ruder, M., & Erb, H. P. (2002). When expertise backfires: Contrast and assimilation effects in persuasion. *British Journal of Social Psychology, 41*(4), 495–519.

Briñol, P., & Petty, R. E. (2009). Source factors in persuasion: A self-validation approach. *European Review of Social Psychology, 20*(1), 49–96.

Chaiken, S., & Eagly, A. H. (1976). Communication modality as a determinant of message persuasiveness and message comprehensibility. *Journal of Personality and Social Psychology, 34*(4), 605–614.

Chaiken, S., & Eagly, A. H. (1983). Communication modality as a determinant of persuasion: The role of communicator salience. *Journal of Personality and Social Psychology, 45*(2), 241–256.

Chen, F. S., Minson, J. A., Schöne, M., & Heinrichs, M. (2013). In the eye of the beholder: Eye contact increases resistance to persuasion. *Psychological Science, 24*(11), 2254–2261.

Cwalina, W., & Koniak, P. (2025). Persuasion. In A. Nai, M. Grömping, & D. Wirz (Eds.), *Elgar encyclopedia of political communication*, vol. 3, pp. 186–190. Cheltenham: Edward Elgar Publishing.

Eaton, A. A., Visser, P. S., & Burns, V. (2017). How gender-role salience influences attitude strength and persuasive message processing. *Psychology of Women Quarterly, 41*(2), 223–239.

Eisend, M. (2006). Two-sided advertising: A meta-analysis. *International Journal of Research in Marketing, 23*(2), 187–198.

Festinger, L. (1957). *A theory of cognitive dissonance.* Stanford, CA: Stanford University Press.

Festinger, L., & Carlsmith, J. M. (1959). Cognitive consequences of forced compliance. *The Journal of Abnormal and Social Psychology, 58*(2), 203–210.

Fujita, K., Eyal, T., Chaiken, S., Trope, Y., & Liberman, N. (2008). Influencing attitudes toward near and distant objects. *Journal of Experimental Social Psychology, 44*(3), 562–572.

Griskevicius, V., Goldstein, N. J., Mortensen, C. R., Sundie, J. M., Cialdini, R. B., & Kenrick, D. T. (2009). Fear and loving in Las Vegas: Evolution, emotion, and persuasion. *Journal of Marketing Research, 46*(3), 384–395.

Guyer, J. J., Vaughan-Johnston, T. I., Fabrigar, L. R., Paredes, B., Briñol, P., & Shen, M. (2025). Vocal speed and processing of persuasive messages: Curvilinear processing effects. *Journal of Nonverbal Behavior, 49*(1), 171–203.

Harmon-Jones, E., & Mills, J. (2019). An introduction to cognitive dissonance theory and an overview of current perspectives on the theory. In E. Harmon-Jones (Ed.), *Cognitive dissonance: Reexamining a pivotal theory in psychology* (2nd ed., pp. 3–24). Washington, DC: American Psychological Association.

Hovland, C. I., Janis, I. L., & Kelley, H. H. (1953). *Communication and persuasion; psychological studies of opinion change*. New Haven, CT: Yale University Press.

Kardes, F. R. (1988). Spontaneous inference processes in advertising: The effects of conclusion omission and involvement on persuasion. *Journal of Consumer Research, 15*(2), 225–233.

Koniak, P., & Cwalina, W. (2022). Forbid/allow asymmetry in persuasion: The forbid frame decreases biased elaboration and increases attitude change. *Social Psychology, 53*(1), 1–20.

Kumkale, G. T., & Albarracín, D. (2004). The sleeper effect in persuasion: A meta-analytic review. *Psychological Bulletin, 130*(1), 143–172.

Kwan, C. M. C., Dai, X., & Wyer, R. S. (2017). Contextual influences on message persuasion: The effect of empty space. *Journal of Consumer Research, 44*(2), 448–464.

Lasswell, H. D. (1948). The structure and function of communication in society. In L. Bryson (Ed.), *The communication of ideas* (pp. 37–51). New York: Harper and Row.

McGuire, W. J. (1968). Personality and attitude change: An information-processing theory. In A. G. Greenwald, T. C. Brock, & T. M. Ostrom (Eds.), *Psychological foundations of attitudes* (pp. 171–196). New York: Academic Press.

McGuire, W. J. (1972). Attitude change: The information processing paradigm. In C. G. McClintock (Ed.), *Experimental social psychology* (pp. 108–141). New York: Holt, Rinehart & Winston.

McGuire, W. J. (2013). McGuire's classic input-output framework for constructing persuasive messages. In R. E. Rice, & C. K. Atkin (Eds.), *Public communication campaigns* (pp. 133–146). Thousand Oaks, CA: Sage Publications.

Pechmann, C. (1992). Predicting when two-sided ads will be more effective than one-sided ads: The role of correlational and correspondent inferences. *Journal of Marketing Research, 29*(4), 441–453.

Petty, R. E., & Cacioppo, J. T. (1990). Involvement and persuasion: Tradition versus integration. *Psychological Bulletin, 107*(3), 367–374.

Petty, R. E., & Wegener, D. T. (1998). Attitude change: Multiple roles for persuasion variables. In D. T. Gilbert, S. T. Fiske, & G. Lindzey (Eds.), *The handbook of social psychology* (4th ed., pp. 323–390). New York: McGraw-Hill.

Rucker, D. D., Petty, R. E., & Briñol, P. (2008). What's in a frame anyway?: A meta-cognitive analysis of the impact of one versus two sided message framing on attitude certainty. *Journal of Consumer Psychology, 18*(2), 137–149.

Schlosser, A. E. (2003). Computers as situational cues: Implications for consumers' product cognitions and attitudes. *Journal of Consumer Psychology, 13*(1–2), 103–112.

Shu, S. B., & Carlson, K. A. (2014). When three charms but four alarms: Identifying the optimal number of claims in persuasion settings. *Journal of Marketing, 78*(1), 127–139.

Van Zant, A. B., & Berger, J. (2020). How the voice persuades. *Journal of Personality and Social Psychology, 118*(4), 661–682.

Visser, P. S., & Krosnick, J. A. (1998). Development of attitude strength over the life cycle: Surge and decline. *Journal of Personality and Social Psychology, 75*(6), 1389–1410.

Wallace, L. E., Wegener, D. T., & Petty, R. E. (2020). When sources honestly provide their biased opinion: Bias as a distinct source perception with independent effects on credibility and persuasion. *Personality and Social Psychology Bulletin, 46*(3), 439–453.

Weaver, K., Garcia, S. M., & Schwarz, N. (2012). The presenter's paradox. *Journal of Consumer Research, 39*(3), 445–460.

Wegener, D. T., Petty, R. E., & Smith, S. M. (1995). Positive mood can increase or decrease message scrutiny: The hedonic contingency view of mood and message processing. *Journal of Personality and Social Psychology, 69*(1), 5–15.

Wood, W., & Quinn, J. M. (2003). Forewarned and forearmed? Two meta-analysis syntheses of forewarnings of influence appeals. *Psychological Bulletin, 129*(1), 119–138.

Zhu, R., & Argo, J. J. (2013). Exploring the impact of various shaped seating arrangements on persuasion. *Journal of Consumer Research, 40*(2), 336–349.

Part 2

Key Theories

This section in summary

- Two mechanisms through which attitudes can influence behaviour, according to the MODE model: the role of motivation and opportunity
- The role of associative and propositional processes in the formation of implicit and explicit attitudes, according to the APE model
- The peripheral/heuristic and central/systematic routes or modes of persuasion, their determinants, and consequences
- The role of resistance in the persuasion process and the factors that increase or decrease it
- The persuasiveness of narratives and the specifics of the transportation process

DOI: 10.4324/9781003589174-7

Chapter 6

Dual-Process and Dual-System Theories of Attitudes

The **dual-process models of attitudes** draw a distinction between a brief and superficial mode of information processing, often assumed to operate under limited resource conditions, and a more thorough, resource-dependent mode (see e.g., Gawronski & Creighton, 2013; Smith & DeCoster, 2000). They are, typically, domain specific and information focused (e.g., attitude change and persuasion, or impression formation). In contrast, **dual-systems model** formulations are more general, process focused, and assumed to apply across domains. They assume that there are two memory systems in the human mind that operate on fundamentally different rules or principles, and not just store different types of information. According to Kahneman (2003, p. 698),

> **Dual-process models**. These models draw a distinction between a fast and superficial mode of information processing, which operates under limited resource conditions, and a more thorough, resource-dependent deliberate mode.
>
> **Dual-system theory**. Theory that assumes that there are two memory systems in the human mind that operate on fundamentally different rules or principles: the operations of System 1 are fast, automatic, effortless, associative, and implicit, and the operations of System 2 are slower, serial, effortful, more likely to be consciously monitored, and deliberately controlled.

> the operations of System 1 are typically fast, automatic, effortless, associative, implicit (not available to introspection), and often emotionally charged; they are also governed by habit and are therefore

DOI: 10.4324/9781003589174-8

difficult to control or modify. The operations of System 2 are slower, serial, effortful, more likely to be consciously monitored and deliberately controlled; they are also relatively flexible and potentially rule governed.

In attitude theory, the dual-process and dual-system ideas have also found expression in theories emphasising two distinct types of processes (associative vs. deliberative or propositional) underlying the formation of evaluative judgements about attitude objects. Examples of such models tested in many research programmes include Fazio's **Motivation and Opportunity as Determinants** (MODE) model and Gawronski and Bodenhausen's Associative-Propositional Evaluation (APE) model.

Motivation and Opportunity as Determinants (MODE) model. It distinguishes two processes underlying the influence of attitudes on behaviour: automatic and deliberative. A deliberative process occurs only when both the motivation and the opportunity for deliberate action exist. In situations where even one of these factors is absent, any effect of attitude on behaviour will operate only through spontaneous processing.

Associative-Propositional Evaluation (APE) model. It distinguishes two qualitatively different types of mental processes: associative and propositional. Associative processes are associated with immediate affective reactions to a given object. Propositional processes, in contrast, underlie evaluative judgements about a given object and determine the validity of these evaluations. The APE model assumes and describes the interaction of these two processes in making evaluative judgements and the conditions under which a given process will dominate.

6.1 The Motivation and Opportunity as Determinants (MODE) Model

The MODE model is based on two mechanisms through which attitudes can influence behaviour (Fazio, 1990; Fazio & Olson, 2014). The difference between them is the degree to which an action is the result of deliberative reflection on the attitude and the degree to which it is a spontaneous reaction without awareness of the underlying attitude. The first of these mechanisms assumes that people consider the consequences of their behaviour before performing it and control it voluntarily. The second mechanism, in contrast, is based on the understanding of attitude as the association in memory between a given object and an evaluation of that object (Fazio, 1986). It is this association strength that determines the accessibility of an attitude and, therefore, the likelihood that it will be automatically or spontaneously activated when an individual encounters its object.

The MODE model provides a way to conceptually integrate the automatic and the deliberative processing of attitude influences on behaviour. Which of these processes occurs depends on both motivation and opportunity. A deliberative process, which consists of retrieving and constructing attitudes towards the behaviour and deciding upon a behavioural intention, occurs only when both the motivation and the opportunity for deliberate action exist. Motivation to exert such effort may arise when an individual's behavioural decision will have serious consequences. When the cost of making a poor decision is high, the individual will be motivated to conduct thorough reasoning, as, for example, in situations characterised by fear of invalidity. As the perceived costs of potential behaviour motivate individuals to exert cognitive effort, the degree to which their attitude towards an object can be automatically activated from memory becomes irrelevant to the behavioural decision-making process. However, the motivation to engage in reasoning alone is not sufficient for it to occur. Favourable opportunities must also arise. For example, deliberation may be significantly limited or even impossible in situations where the individual is under time pressure and must react very quickly.

In situations where motivation is lacking, or where the motivation for deliberation is present but circumstances prevent deeper reflection (e.g., the individual is simultaneously engaged in another activity), any effect of attitude on behaviour will operate only through spontaneous processing. Therefore, only if the object's associations with the evaluation are strong will the encountered object automatically activate the evaluative judgement. The activated attitude can then colour individuals' immediate perceptions and, consequently, influence their behaviour towards that object. However, if the attitudinal association is too weak to be activated, behaviour will be influenced by the nature or context of the event, which is not attitudinally based. Whatever features of the attitude object and the situational cues will attract individuals' attention, they will serve as the basis for perceptions and behaviour.

An overall attitude-to-behaviour process that is essentially deliberative in nature may still involve some elements that are automatised. And conversely, the essentially spontaneous process itself sometimes involves some components that are controlled. Nevertheless, these processes can be generally divided into two basic classes: the spontaneous sequence and the deliberative sequence.

In a test of the MODE model, Sanbonmatsu and Fazio (1990) provided participants with information about two different department stores. The description suggested that one store (Smith's) was generally better stocked. However, the second store (Brown's) was presented with statements suggesting it had a better camera department. Participants had to evaluate which store they would visit to purchase a camera. The aim of the experiment was to distinguish under which conditions participants would make an effort to search their memory for previously obtained detailed information about the camera department of each store, rather than simply relying on their own feelings about which store was better. The participants' motivation to make the correct decision was manipulated by telling some of them that they would have to justify their choice to a group of students and the experimenter (high motivation). The remaining participants were simply asked to choose which store they would purchase a camera from (low motivation). Additionally, some subjects were forced to make decisions quickly (time pressure), while the rest could do so at their own pace (no time pressure).

The experimental results were consistent with the predictions derived from the MODE model. When participants were motivated and given the opportunity to make a choice, they chose Brown's because it had a better camera section. Only when motivation and opportunity were high did participants make the effort necessary to recall specific details from memory. When they were either less motivated or under time pressure, they made their decision based on their overall attitude and chose Smith's.

In summary, according to the MODE model, the process described by the theory of reasoned action is more likely to occur when the situation both motivates the individual to carefully consider an action and provides the opportunity to do so. Without these factors, the spontaneous process described by Fazio (1986) is more likely.

6.2 The Associative-Propositional Evaluation (APE) Model

The APE model was developed by Gawronski and Bodenhausen (2006, 2007, 2014). It is based on earlier dual-process theories of cognitive functioning, which distinguish two qualitatively different types of mental processes: associative processes, which underlie **implicit attitudes**, and propositional processes, which underlie **explicit attitudes** (see Chapter 1). An attitude is understood here as a general evaluative tendency towards an object, which stems from these two types of processes and their interplay. **Associative processes** underlie immediate affective reactions to a given object. Whether these reactions are positive or negative depends on the specific associations activated in response to it. A main factor activating this process is the similarity between the features of encountered stimuli and existing mental representations. Concept activation can then spread to other concepts that are associatively linked in memory. It is not an all-or-none process, such that encountering a given object would activate each and every concept that is associated with that object in memory. Moreover, for the activation of associations it is not important whether the evaluative judgements that result from them are accurate or not. **Propositional processes** are a second source of evaluative tendencies. They underlie endorsed evaluative judgements about a given object. According to the APE model, the goal of propositional reasoning processes is to establish the validity of evaluations and beliefs by assessing their consistency with other relevant propositions that are momentarily considered relevant to a given judgement. Thus, the most important feature distinguishing propositional from associative processes is their dependence on truth values.

According to the APE model, the fact that associative and propositional processes are qualitatively distinct does not mean that they are mutually independent. Associative processes can influence propositional processes, such that the affective reactions resulting from activated associations provide inputs for processes of propositional reasoning characterised by the **validation** of evaluations and beliefs. However, propositional processes can impact associative processes by activating particular associations in memory, and may also influence affective responses by creating new associations. However, the more propositions a person considers for an evaluative judgement, the more likely it becomes that the propositional translation of an affective reaction is inconsistent with other relevant propositions, and thus will be rejected as a basis for the judgement.

Furthermore, the APE model identifies four basic scenarios for how an external object can influence implicit and explicit evaluations and change them. In the first scenario, an external stimulus activates associations, and the resulting evaluation is accepted by propositional validation. This leads to corresponding changes in both implicit and explicit evaluations, with explicit changes mediated by implicit ones. An example is evaluative conditioning, where participants focus on their feelings. The second scenario refers to a situation where associative processes are activated, but the resulting evaluation is rejected in the propositional validation process. According to the APE model, this results in changes in implicit but not explicit evaluations. An example is evaluative conditioning, where participants reflect on prior knowledge, overriding the implicit response. The next two scenarios assume that an external factor activates propositional processes. In the first scenario, this does not influence the activation of associations. This leads to changes in explicit but not implicit evaluations, as is the case, for example, with cognitive dissonance. However, induced propositional validation processes can also influence associations. This, in turn, causes corresponding changes in both implicit and explicit evaluations, with implicit changes mediated by explicit ones. Acquiring new propositional information (e.g., about a person's behaviour) is an example.

The APE model also qualifies some common assumptions about implicit and explicit evaluations and the nature of their underlying mental entities. First, the model assumes that people generally (although not necessarily) do have some degree of conscious access to their affective, and that they tend to rely on these reactions when making evaluative judgements. However, even if people may be consciously aware of the affective reactions, they may be unaware of the associative processes that lead to these reactions. Second, affective reactions do not require intention to get activated, although they can get activated intentionally. Third, affective reactions do not require much cognitive capacity to get activated, although they can get activated by effortful processes. Finally, whether affective reactions can be successfully controlled depends on the nature of the adopted control strategy.

Further Readings

Gawronski, B., & Creighton, L. A. (2013). Dual process theories. In D. E. Carlston (Ed.), *The Oxford handbook of social cognition* (pp. 282–312). New York: Oxford University Press.

Smith, E. R., & DeCoster, J. (2000). Dual-process models in social and cognitive psychology: Conceptual integration and links to underlying memory systems. *Personality and Social Psychology Review*, *4*(2), 108–131.

References

Fazio, R. H. (1986). How do attitudes guide behavior? In R. M. Sorrentino & E. T. Higgins (Eds.), *Handbook of motivation and cognition: Foundations of social behavior* (pp. 204–243). New York: Guilford Press.

Fazio, R. H. (1990). Multiple processes by which attitudes guide behavior: The MODE model as an integrative framework. In M. E. Zanna (Ed.), *Advances in in experimental social psychology* (Vol. 23, pp. 75–109). New York: Academic Press.

Fazio, R. H., & Olson, M. A. (2014). The MODE model: Attitude-behavior processes as a function of motivation and opportunity. In J. W. Sherman, B. Gawronski, & Y. Trope (Eds.), *Dual-process theories of the social mind* (pp. 155–171). New York: Guilford Press.

Gawronski, B., & Bodenhausen, G. V. (2006). Associative and propositional processes in evaluation: An integrative review of implicit and explicit attitude change. *Psychological Bulletin*, *132*(5), 692–731.

Gawronski, B., & Bodenhausen, G. V. (2007). Unraveling the process underlying evaluation: Attitudes from the perspective of the APE model. *Social Cognition*, *25*(5), 687–717.

Gawronski, B., & Bodenhausen, G. V. (2014). Implicit and explicit evaluation: A brief review of the associative-propositional evaluation model. *Social and Personality Psychology Compass*, *8*(8), 448–462.

Gawronski, B., & Creighton, L. A. (2013). Dual process theories. In D. E. Carlston (Ed.), *The Oxford handbook of social cognition* (pp. 282–312). New York: Oxford University Press.

Kahneman, D. (2003). A perspective on judgment and choice: Mapping bounded rationality. *American Psychologist, 58*(9), 697–720.

Sanbonmatsu, D. M., & Fazio, R. H. (1990). The role of attitudes in memory–based decision making. *Journal of Personality and Social Psychology, 59*(4), 614–622.

Smith, E. R., & DeCoster, J. (2000). Dual-process models in social and cognitive psychology: Conceptual integration and links to underlying memory systems. *Personality and Social Psychology Review*, *4*(2), 108–131.

Chapter 7

Dual-Process Theories of Attitude Formation and Change

Since the mid-20th-century resurgence of interest in persuasion, researchers have described the various processes involved in forming and changing attitudes. These processes can be classified as either requiring relatively little cognitive effort on the part of the recipient or requiring more effort and thought. Relatively effortless processes include evaluative conditioning and mere exposure (see Sections 3.2 and 3.4). Those requiring more effort from the recipient are based on understanding and evaluating the arguments presented. According to the cognitive response approach, the effectiveness of persuasion depends on active thought about the object of persuasion (as well as the source, message, etc.). When confronted with a persuasive message, the receiver engages in counterargumentation and/or approval thoughts (**cognitive response model**; Greenwald, 1968). Dual-process theories of attitude formation and change describe the circumstances in which persuasion is based on one process or the other, and the consequences for attitudes stemming from this.

7.1 The Elaboration Likelihood Model (ELM)

The ELM of persuasion is the most widely studied dual-process model of attitude formation and change. Created by Richard E. Petty and John Cacioppo (1986a, 1986b), it has since been developed by them and their collaborators (e.g., Petty & Briñol, 2012; Petty & Wegener, 1999). **Elaboration** relates to the effort people put into processing information, thinking about it, and comparing it with their existing knowledge. It can be considered as a continuum ranging from very low to very high. The model describes **two routes to persuasion**: The **peripheral route** is based on low-effort processing. The **central**

Elaboration. The effort people put into processing information, thinking about it, and comparing it with their existing knowledge.

DOI: 10.4324/9781003589174-9

route is related to persuasion based mostly on elaboration. However, the two routes are not entirely distinct. As elaboration increases, the central route becomes more prevalent, while the peripheral route becomes less significant. In most cases, both routes are at play, and the question is which one dominates. Furthermore, at medium levels of elaboration, the two routes play a similar role.

Peripheral route to persuasion. Formation or change of attitudes based on low-effort processing, mostly on peripheral cues present in the given persuasive situation, rather than on the elaboration of arguments.

Central route to persuasion. Formation or change of attitudes based on high-effort processing, elaboration of arguments and receiver's cognitive responses.

7.1.1 Determinants of Elaboration

The **likelihood of elaboration** depends on two categories of variables: **motivation** and the **ability** to process information. These variables may be influenced by the individual traits of the recipient, as well as by the situation (e.g., who the source is, what the message is about, and previous events). One important **motivational factor** is how **relevant** or **important** the message is to the recipient. As the relevance or importance of the issue increases, so does elaboration. Therefore, persuasion is mostly based on the peripheral route when the topic is irrelevant or unimportant, and on the central route when the issue is relevant or important. For example, many studies have demonstrated that relevance and importance can be increased by informing student participants that an educational reform in the senior comprehensive exams will be implemented the following year. Conversely, low relevance or importance can be achieved by informing them that the reform will be implemented in ten years (Petty et al., 1981). Another motivational variable is the **Need for Cognition (NFC)**, which is a relatively stable trait, though not an invariable one. It refers to an individual's "tendency to engage in and enjoy effortful cognitive activity" (Cacioppo et al., 1996, p. 198). This can be measured using the Need for Cognition Scale, for which both long and short versions are available (see Cacioppo et al., 1996). People with a high NFC engage in greater elaboration than those with a low NFC, and as a result, persuasion is more related to central route processes in the former group. Another motivational factor is **personal responsibility**: elaboration likelihood is lower when people are part of a group responsible for a task (e.g., choosing an offer or evaluating an editorial) than when they are responsible individually (Petty et al., 1980).

Examples of **ability-related** variables include the receiver's characteristics, such as their intelligence, which is distinct from NFC. Another variable in this group is the receiver's prior **knowledge** of the message's subject matter. People with a high level of topic- or object-relevant knowledge elaborate the message more than those with a low level of this knowledge (Wood et al., 1995). However, **variables external to the receiver** can also influence their ability to elaborate. **Repeating** the message can provide an opportunity to process points that were previously missed (although repeating can also have some drawbacks – see Section 11.1.1). **Distractors**, such as noise or additional tasks, are events or tasks that coincide with the focal message. They generally reduce elaboration and reliance on the central route. This is due to a reduction in processing resources and is therefore related to ability. However, **interruptions** – events or tasks that temporarily prevent the recipient from completing message processing, such as a pause while a video loads or someone asking for help while the recipient is reading a message – can increase elaboration when processing resumes. This effect is the result of increased curiosity, which is related to motivational factors (Kupor & Tormala, 2015). Another example is **message comprehensibility**. Elaboration is lower for difficult-to-comprehend messages (e.g., use of jargon, rare words, and/or complex grammatical structures) than for easier-to-comprehend messages (e.g., use of lay terminology, no rare words, and/or complex grammatical structures; Hafer et al., 1996). It should be noted that difficult-to-understand message may affect the likelihood of elaboration by reducing both processing ability and motivation to process.

Need for Cognition (NFC). Relatively stable individual's tendency to engage in and enjoy effortful cognitive activity.

Distractors. Events or tasks that coincide with the focal message, such as noise or additional tasks.

Interruptions. Events or tasks that temporarily prevent the recipient from completing message processing, such as a pause while a video loads or someone asking for help while the recipient is reading a message.

7.1.2 Two Routes of Persuasion

When both motivation and ability are high, persuasion is based on the **central route**. In this case, it is the receiver's cognitive responses that determine the change in attitude. These **cognitive responses** are the

> **Cognitive responses**. Thoughts generated by the receiver while they are confronted with attitude-relevant information.

thoughts generated by the receiver while they are exposed to the persuasive message. They may focus on the topic of persuasion and the essence of the argument, or they may focus on other aspects, such as the style of the message, the characteristics of the source or completely unrelated things (e.g., last night's dinner). Topic- or message-related thoughts may support or challenge the arguments presented. The direction of the attitude change depends on which type of topic-related cognitive response prevails. One way to measure cognitive reactions is the **thought-listing technique**. After a message has been presented, respondents are asked to list all the thoughts that occurred to them while reading or listening to it. These thoughts are then coded by independent raters or by the respondents themselves. These thoughts can be categorised into various distinct groups, such as supportive, counter-argumentative, or neutral. Depending on the objective, they can also be classified as being related to the source, the message, and so on. These coded thoughts can then be combined to create an index of thought positivity by subtracting the number of negative thoughts from the number of positive ones (see Cacioppo & Petty, 1981).

Thus, in the central route, receivers persuade themselves through their own thoughts. Persuasive communication may encourage them to elaborate on the topic, for example, by highlighting its importance and not hindering the processing of the message. However, it may also influence or push the cognitive responses of the receiver in a desired direction. The primary means of shaping the direction of the receiver's cognitive response is the **quality of the arguments** (see Sections 5.3.2 and 12.1). Strong arguments lead to thoughts that are consistent with the persuasive goal (e.g., favourable thoughts if the goal is to persuade someone that an object is good), while thoughts that are inconsistent with the goal (e.g., unfavourable thoughts) are suppressed. Conversely, weak arguments lead to thoughts that are predominantly inconsistent with the persuasive goal.

Note that increased elaboration does not necessarily lead to greater persuasive effectiveness. In fact, a weak message may be more persuasive when elaboration is low than when it is high, since low-elaborating receivers will not generate as many negative thoughts as high-elaborating receivers when presented with a weak message. This can lead to seemingly paradoxical consequences: for instance, distractors may both increase and decrease persuasive effectiveness. Distractors may boost persuasiveness when arguments are weak and distraction hinders the formation of counterarguments. However, they may reduce it when arguments are strong and distraction hinders the generation of supportive thoughts.

Peripheral cue. A factor unrelated to the merit of an argument that can be used to form or change attitudes with low elaboration.

Manipulating the quality of arguments or messages is a **methodological tool** that can be used to assess the scope of elaboration and its relationship with other variables. For example, to examine the impact of personal relevance on elaboration, one group of participants could be led to view an issue as highly relevant, while another group could be led to view it as rather irrelevant. Next, these two groups would each be divided into two subgroups, one of which would receive a strong message and the other a weak one. If personal relevance increases elaboration likelihood, then participants in the high relevance group should be more persuaded by strong arguments than those in the low relevance group. Conversely, the weak message should elicit more negative attitudes from the high relevance group than from the low relevance group. In other words, the difference in attitudes after receiving strong and weak messages should be greater when elaboration is high than when it is low.

The ELM central route describes the ideal conditions for elaboration. However, those who receive a persuasive message are not always motivated or able to process it extensively. This does not necessarily mean that they will postpone forming an attitude, since one of the ELM's basic assumptions is that "people are motivated to hold correct attitudes" (Petty & Cacioppo, 1986b, p. 127). When lacking motivation and/or ability, therefore, people base their attitudes not on extensive elaboration of the arguments in the message, but on various simple cues present in the given persuasive situation. This is known as the **peripheral route of persuasion**. For instance, individuals may adopt a favourable view of the subject of persuasion merely because it is endorsed by an attractive source. Alternatively, they may develop a negative attitude simply because the source is seen as untrustworthy. Many other variables may serve as **peripheral cues**, such as the number of arguments (see Section 5.3.2) or the receiver's positive or negative emotions, even if these emotions result from sources unrelated to the persuasion. The influence of the peripheral route can also be observed when the central route does not result in a predominance of positive or negative thoughts.

7.1.3 Objective versus Biased Processing

The ELM assumes that elaboration can be more or less biased, and that this bias can be either motivated or ability-based. For instance, a person's initial attitude towards a persuasive object can influence the direction or valence of their thoughts by biasing the way they process information about that object. People tend to perceive arguments or information that are consistent with their attitudes as stronger than inconsistent ones. Furthermore, having prior knowledge of the issue enables individuals to counterargue messages that are inconsistent with their pre-existing attitudes. Another example is when the receiver is forewarned of the speaker's persuasive intent. This motivates the receiver to counterargue the presented arguments, even when they are strong and without the forewarning, the receiver would be effectively persuaded by them.

7.1.4 Multiple Roles of Variables

Although variables such as the source's characteristics or the receiver's emotional state act as cues in the peripheral route of persuasion, this does not mean that these variables are irrelevant in the central route of processing. According to the ELM, each variable can fulfil one of several persuasive roles. First, when elaboration is low, they may serve as **peripheral cues**. For instance, an expert source may influence the attitude towards the object of persuasion by enabling agreement with the conclusion without the need for further thought. Similarly, pleasant music in an advertisement may influence the attitude towards the product through evaluative conditioning (see Section 3.4). Second, the same variable can be used as an **argument**. When the level of elaboration is high, the expertise of the source can provide an additional reason for the proposed solutions. Or, for example, pleasant music in an advertisement for a new film may be another reason to see it. Third, each variable can potentially **affect the scope of elaboration**. Some people are more interested in what experts say and will process messages from expert sources more thoroughly than those who are more interested in what attractive sources say (see Section 12.1.1). Pleasant music can distract the recipient from processing the advertisement if they are trying to recall the song's title. Fourth, a variable can affect the **direction of cognitive responses**. For instance, if the recipient is a conspiracy theorist who does not trust experts, they may argue against the expert's opinion. Similarly, pleasant music in an advert may elicit positive cognitive responses.

7.1.5 Self-Validation Theory (SVT)

Variables can also play a fifth, metacognitive, role in persuasion. **Metacognition** refers to people's thoughts about their own thought processes. For example, they may consider whether they have given a particular issue sufficient thought. Alternatively, they may suspect that their thoughts

> **Metacognitive processes (metacognition)**. People's thoughts about their own thought processes.

are the result of suggestions. This concept is explored in Self-Validation Theory (Briñol & Petty, 2022) and has applications beyond persuasion. However, as it emerged from research extending the ELM, it will only be mentioned briefly here. SVT's fundamental principle is that the impact of thoughts on attitudes (as well as beliefs, goals, decisions, and behaviours) depends on their **perceived validity**. Here, what matters is not whether the thoughts are objectively valid, but whether an individual perceives them as such. Thus, thoughts perceived as more valid become more consequential.

Our thoughts can be **validated** in two ways: **cognitively**, when we believe them to be correct representations of reality, and **affectively**, when we feel good about them or simply like them. This validation may result from various factors, including incidental factors related to the thoughts themselves, such as our emotional state, physical actions (e.g., handwashing), and body posture. For instance, horizontal head movements (e.g., shaking the head from side to side to indicate "no") have been found to be associated with lower perceived thought validity than vertical movements (e.g., nodding to indicate "yes"). Consequently, the impact of these thoughts on attitudes is reduced (Briñol & Petty, 2003). Similarly, information about the credibility of the source may influence how thoughts are perceived. When such information precedes a message and the level of elaboration is relatively high, the credibility of the source affects the valence of issue-relevant thinking. In this situation, particularly when the message itself is neither unambiguously positive nor negative, receivers' thoughts tend to align more with the direction of the argument if the source is credible. However, when this information follows the message, it influences how confident people are about the thoughts they have just generated. Those told that the author of a message is highly credible have more confidence in their thoughts than those told that the message comes from a low-credibility source (Tormala et al., 2007).

When variables increase or decrease the perceived validity of thoughts, the consequences for attitudes depend on the valence of those thoughts. Increasing confidence in thoughts that are consistent with the persuasive message (e.g., when strong arguments are used) increases persuasiveness. Conversely, decreasing confidence decreases persuasiveness. However, when thoughts that are inconsistent with the persuasive message prevail (e.g., due to weak argumentation), increasing confidence in these thoughts decreases persuasiveness, whereas decreasing confidence has the opposite effect (Briñol & Petty, 2003; Tormala et al., 2007).

7.1.6 The Consequences of the Persuasion Route

If adequate cues and/or argumentation are available, both routes of persuasion can result in attitudes that are similar in terms of valence and confidence. However, these attitudes have different properties. In the central route, cognitions related to the object of persuasion are formed and stored in a person's cognitive structures. Attitudes formed or changed via the central route are more **persistent** than those formed or changed via the peripheral route, that is, they decay less over time and will maintain their valence. They are also more **resistant** to counter-persuasion, that is, messages that attempt to change attitudes in the opposite direction. People who formed an attitude via the central route actively counterargue such messages. Conversely, attitudes formed via the peripheral route are susceptible to such attacks; people who formed their attitudes via this route simply agree with the new message and adjust their attitude accordingly (Haugtvedt & Petty, 1992). Furthermore, attitudes formed via the central route are more **predictive of behaviour** than those formed via the peripheral route (Cacioppo et al., 1986).

7.2 The Heuristic–Systematic Model (HSM)

Another prominent dual-process theory of persuasion is the Heuristic–Systematic Model (HSM), developed by Shelly Chaiken and her colleagues (Chaiken, 1980; Chaiken et al., 1989). Similar to the ELM, the HSM describes two modes of persuasion, and its conceptualisation of the high processing mode ("systematic processing") is similar to that of the ELM. The HSM also shares a similar view of the antecedents and consequences of this processing mode (Eagly & Chaiken, 1993). Therefore, we will only address the main differences between the two models here.

7.2.1 *Heuristic Processing*

This processing mode requires less effort and fewer cognitive resources than systematic processing. In **systematic processing**, the receiver analyses and comprehensively processes information, checking its relevance to the judgement task at hand. In **heuristic processing**, people focus on a relatively small subset of the available information (**heuristic cues**). This information enables the use of simple decision rules, or cognitive heuristics, to make judgements, decisions, or form

Systematic processing. Comprehensive processing and analysis of the information, checking its relevance to the judgement task at hand.

Heuristic processing. Basing the judgement, decision, or attitude on a relatively small subset of the available information, allowing for the implementation of simple decision rules (heuristic cues).

attitudes. Examples of such heuristics include "expert statements are valid" when the message comes from an expert source, and "consensus implies correctness" when the message is presented as supported by the majority. Therefore, this low-effort mode of persuasion is more narrowly defined here than in the ELM, where peripheral cues can operate through a wide range of mechanisms, such as evaluative conditioning.

Heuristic cue. Any element of a persuasive situation that enables the use of simple decision-making rules or cognitive heuristics to make judgements, decisions, or form attitudes.

Additionally, the HSM predicts which heuristic cues are likely to be more persuasive. Heuristic cues are generally considered to be more effective when the associated heuristic is more **accessible**. This accessibility may depend on the persuasive situation or channel (Chaiken & Eagly, 1983; see Section 5.3.3). It may also be a chronic characteristic of the recipients. For example, some individuals may use the "length implies strength" heuristic more often than others and consequently be more inclined to agree with messages containing a greater number of arguments than those with fewer arguments (see Eagly & Chaiken, 1993). Furthermore, people should use the heuristics that they subjectively perceive to be **reliable**. For instance, if receivers are sufficiently motivated, they may place greater reliance on information about consensus based on a large survey than on a small pool of respondents (Darke et al., 1998).

7.2.2 Determinants of Processing Mode

Similar to ELM, HSM assumes that systematic processing demands and consumes cognitive capacity. However, HSM uniquely addresses motivational determinants of processing. According to this model, people want to achieve their goals in the most efficient way possible with the least effort. Consequently, they often prefer heuristic to systematic processing. However, they are also motivated by the desire to have accurate attitudes, so they try to strike a balance between satisfying their motivational needs and minimising processing effort. They will make as much effort as is required until they have achieved a sufficient degree of confidence in their attitudes. The **sufficiency threshold** (ST) is the level of confidence desired by an individual in a given situation. This ST may vary between individuals and may also differ for the same person depending on the attitude, object, or situation.

Sufficiency threshold (ST). The level of confidence desired by an individual in a given situation.

If the **actual level of confidence** (AC) attained by an individual falls below the ST, it is deemed insufficient. Therefore, processing effort should cease when AC equals or exceeds ST. In other words, processing effort is a function of the discrepancy between AC and ST.

Accuracy motivation. Desire to develop valid attitudes based on facts.

Defence motivation. Desire to form or defend a specific attitude.

Impression motivation. Desire to display socially acceptable attitudes.

7.2.3 Multiple Motives

According to HSM, processing may be driven by three types of motivation: accuracy, defence, and impression. An **accuracy-motivated** receiver assesses the validity of information relevant to attitudes in order to develop valid attitudes based on facts. **Defence motivation** is the desire to form or defend a specific attitude. This can be influenced by various factors, such as value-relevant involvement, vested interest, or commitment to a specific attitude (see Chapter 8). **Impression motivation** reflects the desire to display socially acceptable attitudes. It is especially activated when an individual believes they are being evaluated by significant others, when social relations are at stake, or when an individual needs to justify their attitudes to others. While accuracy-motivated processing is considered relatively open-minded and unbiased, defence and impression motivations tend to be more closed-minded, biased, and selective. All of these motives can be satisfied through systematic or heuristic processing. The sufficiency principle also applies to each of them.

7.2.4 Concurrent Processing Assumption (Co-occurrence Hypotheses)

According to HSM, the heuristic processing mode begins to operate at low levels of motivation and ability, and continues to do so as processing efforts increase. Therefore, at high levels of processing, persuasion relies on the two modes described by this model. Consequently, the impact of heuristic and systematic processing on persuasion may be either independent (additive) or interdependent (interactive). These relationships can be described using four co-occurrence hypotheses (Bohner et al., 1995; Chaiken & Maheswaran, 1994; Maheswaran & Chaiken, 1991). First, the effects of heuristic and systematic processing may be independent and additive (**the additivity hypothesis**). This is typically observed when individuals are motivated to engage in processing, and when the effects of heuristic and systematic processing are not contradictory (e.g., information indicating that the majority of consumers favour a specific product, coupled with a message presenting it as superior to competing brands). In this situation, motivated receivers base their attitudes on both attribute-related thoughts (treated as an index of systematic processing) and perceived consensus (heuristic processing).

Second, the effects of heuristic processing are often attenuated by systematic processing (**the attenuation hypothesis**). This occurs when the results of systematic processing contradict the validity of heuristic processing (e.g., when most consumers prefer a product presented as inferior to competing brands). In this situation, perceived consensus does not affect the attitudes of highly motivated respondents. Third, the two processing modes may interact in such a way that **heuristic processing biases systematic processing**. This occurs when recipients are motivated or have sufficient resources, but the message contains ambiguous information (e.g., the recommended product is superior to the competing brand in half of the presented attributes but inferior in the other half). Here, expectations based on heuristic processing can influence respondents' cognitive responses and resulting attitudes, making them more positive in the presence of a positive heuristic cue (e.g., credible sources) and more negative in the presence of a negative heuristic cue (e.g., non-credible sources).

Fourth, expectations based on heuristic processing may be **violated** by systematic processing effects. This can lead to **contrasting cognitive reactions to the value of expectations**. Therefore, disconfirmation of positive expectations results in a **negative processing bias**, whereas disconfirmation of negative expectations results in a **positive processing bias**. For instance, recipients may express less favourable thoughts and attitudes after reading weak arguments presented by an expert than after reading the same arguments presented by a layperson. Conversely, they may report more favourable thoughts after reading strong arguments presented by a layperson than after reading the same arguments presented by an expert (Bohner et al., 2002).

Further Readings

Chaiken, S., Liberman, A., & Eagly, A. H. (1989). Heuristic and systematic information processing within and beyond the persuasion context. In J. S. Uleman, & J. A. Bargh (Eds.), *Unintended thought* (pp. 212–252). New York: Guilford Press.

Petty, R. E., & Cacioppo, J. T. (1986). The elaboration likelihood model of persuasion. In L. Berkowitz (Ed.), *Advances in experimental social psychology* (Vol. 19, pp. 123–205). New York: Academic Press.

References

Bohner, G., Moskowitz, G. B., & Chaiken, S. (1995). The interplay of heuristic and systematic processing of social information. *European Review of Social Psychology, 6*(1), 33–68.

Bohner, G., Ruder, M., & Erb, H. P. (2002). When expertise backfires: Contrast and assimilation effects in persuasion. *British Journal of Social Psychology, 41*(4), 495–519.

Briñol, P., & Petty, R. E. (2003). Overt head movements and persuasion: A self-validation analysis. *Journal of Personality and Social Psychology, 84*(6), 1123–1139.

Briñol, P., & Petty, R. E. (2022). Self-validation theory: An integrative framework for understanding when thoughts become consequential. *Psychological Review, 129*(2), 340–367.

Cacioppo, J. T., & Petty, R. E. (1981). Social psychological procedures for cognitive response assessment: The thought listing technique. In T. Merluzzi, C. Glass, & M. Genest (Eds.), *Cognitive assessment* (pp. 309–342). New York: Guilford Press.

Cacioppo, J. T., Petty, R. E., Feinstein, J. A., & Jarvis, W. B. G. (1996). Dispositional differences in cognitive motivation: The life and times of individuals varying in need for cognition. *Psychological Bulletin, 119*(2), 197–253.

Cacioppo, J. T., Petty, R. E., Kao, C. F., & Rodriguez, R. (1986). Central and peripheral routes to persuasion: An individual difference perspective. *Journal of Personality and Social Psychology, 51*(5), 1032–1043.

Chaiken, S. (1980). Heuristic versus systematic information processing and the use of source versus message cues in persuasion. *Journal of Personality and Social Psychology, 39*(5), 752–766.

Chaiken, S., & Eagly, A. H. (1983). Communication modality as a determinant of persuasion: The role of communicator salience. *Journal of Personality and Social Psychology, 45*(2), 241–256.

Chaiken, S., Liberman, A., & Eagly, A. H. (1989). Heuristic and systematic information processing within and beyond the persuasion context. In J. S. Uleman, & J. A. Bargh (Eds.), *Unintended thought* (pp. 212–252). New York: Guilford Press.

Chaiken, S., & Maheswaran, D. (1994). Heuristic processing can bias systematic processing: Effects of source credibility, argument ambiguity, and task importance on attitude judgment. *Journal of Personality and Social Psychology, 66*(3), 460–473.

Darke, P. R., Chaiken, S., Bohner, G., Einwiller, S., Erb, H. P., & Hazlewood, J. D. (1998). Accuracy motivation, consensus information, and the law of large numbers: Effects on attitude judgment in the absence of argumentation. *Personality and Social Psychology Bulletin, 24*(11), 1205–1215.

Eagly, A. H., & Chaiken, S. (1993). *The psychology of attitudes.* Fort Worth, TX: Harcourt Brace Jovanovich College Publishers.

Greenwald, A. G. (1968). Cognitive learning, cognitive response to persuasion, and attitude change. In A. G. Greenwald, T. C. Brock, & T. M. Ostrom (Eds.), *Psychological foundations of attitudes* (pp. 147–170). New York: Academic Press.

Hafer, C. L., Reynolds, K. L., & Obertynski, M. A. (1996). Message comprehensibility and persuasion: Effects of complex language in counterattitudinal appeals to laypeople. *Social Cognition, 14*(4), 317–337.

Haugtvedt, C. P., & Petty, R. E. (1992). Personality and persuasion: Need for cognition moderates the persistence and resistance of attitude changes. *Journal of Personality and Social Psychology, 63*(2), 308–319.

Kupor, D. M., & Tormala, Z. L. (2015). Persuasion, interrupted: The effect of momentary interruptions on message processing and persuasion. *Journal of Consumer Research, 42*(2), 300–315.

Maheswaran, D., & Chaiken, S. (1991). Promoting systematic processing in low-motivation settings: Effect of incongruent information on processing and judgment. *Journal of Personality and Social Psychology, 61*(1), 13–25.

Petty, R. E., & Briñol, P. (2012). The elaboration likelihood model. In P. A. Van Lange, A. W. Kruglanski, & E. T. Higgins (Eds.), *Handbook of theories of social psychology* (Vol. 1, pp. 224–245). Thousand Oaks, CA: Sage Publications.

Petty, R. E., & Cacioppo, J. T. (1986a). *Communication and persuasion: Central and peripheral routes to attitude change.* New York: Springer-Verlag.

Petty, R. E., & Cacioppo, J. T. (1986b). The elaboration likelihood model of persuasion. In L. Berkowitz (Ed.), *Advances in experimental social psychology* (Vol. 19, pp. 123–205). New York: Academic Press.

Petty, R. E., Cacioppo, J. T., & Goldman, R. (1981). Personal involvement as a determinant of argument-based persuasion. *Journal of Personality and Social Psychology, 41*(5), 847–855.

Petty, R. E., Harkins, S. G., & Williams, K. D. (1980). The effects of group diffusion of cognitive effort on attitudes: An information-processing view. *Journal of Personality and Social Psychology, 38*(1), 81–92.

Petty, R. E., & Wegener, D. T. (1999). The elaboration likelihood model: Current status and controversies. In S. Chaiken, & Y. Trope (Eds.), *Dual-process theories in social psychology* (pp. 37–72). New York: Guilford Press.

Tormala, Z. L., Briñol, P., & Petty, R. E. (2007). Multiple roles for source credibility under high elaboration: It's all in the timing. *Social Cognition, 25*(4), 536–552.

Wood, W., Rhodes, N., & Biek, M. (1995). Working knowledge and attitude strength: An information-processing analysis. In R. E. Petty, & J. A. Krosnick (Eds.), *Attitude strength: Antecedents and consequences* (pp. 283–313). Hillsdale, NJ: Lawrence Erlbaum Associates.

Chapter 8

Theories and Models of Resistance to Persuasion

People often react with resistance when they are persuaded to adopt an opinion or take an action. This resistance can stem from various aspects of the persuasive situation. First, the fact of being persuaded, if perceived as such, can trigger such a reaction in itself. Second, the style, language, or other features of the communication, such as the number of arguments or repetitions, may encourage people to resist. Third, resistance may be triggered by a discrepancy between incoming information and the recipient's pre-existing attitudes.

The concept of resistance is also embedded in the aforementioned models of persuasion. The ELM describes how pre-existing attitudes or forewarning of persuasive intent can result in biased processing (see Section 7.1). The HSM states that processing can be driven by defensive motivation (see Section 7.2). In this chapter, however, we will focus on theories and models that primarily address resistance itself.

It should be noted that, while resistance can be an obstacle to persuasion, it can also be desirable, for example, when we want to ensure that counterpersuasion will not work. The dual models of persuasion also describe how to reduce the effectiveness of counterpersuasion. These models assume that attitudes formed or changed via the central/systematic route are stronger and more resistant to attacking messages (see Section 7.1). Resistance can also be a useful defence against malevolent persuasion, propaganda, and fake news. Thus, the goal of persuasion is sometimes to prepare people in advance to resist or inoculate them against future counterpersuasion attempts (we will return to this in Section 12.4). However, such resistance or defensiveness can hinder positive persuasion, for example, when trying to persuade people to undergo regular health checks. It can also hinder democratic processes and the exchange and discussion of ideas (see Section 12.3).

DOI: 10.4324/9781003589174-10

8.1 Psychological Reactance Theory

According to psychological reactance theory (Brehm, 1966; Brehm & Brehm, 1981), people believe that they are free to do, feel, or think whatever they want, and that they are free to develop and maintain their own attitudes and opinions. When this freedom is perceived as being threatened, whether or not the threat actually exists, an unpleasant state known as **reactance** is experienced. Reactance may also result from reading about, listening to, or observing threats to the freedom of others (known as **vicarious reactance**), even when the threat is not directed at the individual experiencing reactance. However, this kind of reactance is less impulsive and emotional and more reflective and cognitive in nature than reactance resulting from a direct threat (Steindl et al., 2015).

Psychological reactance can be described as a state of mixed cognition and emotion, involving negative cognitive responses such as counterargumentation, as well as anger (Dillard & Shen, 2005). It motivates people to try to restore threatened freedom. This **restoration** may be direct, for example, by doing what is perceived as forbidden (the **boomerang effect**, e.g., increasing the legal drinking age could lead to younger students drinking more). However, restoration is often more indirect. People can restore the freedom they feel is threatened by increasing their preference for the threatened choice (making the forbidden fruit more appealing, e.g., by perceiving phosphate detergents as more efficient after they were banned), or by downgrading the imposed option (e.g., being forced to eat vegetables instead of sweets, resulting in a decreased preference for fruit). They may also evaluate the source of the threat negatively (e.g., a doctor telling them to stop smoking), deny that the threat exists (e.g., believing that coronavirus is not a serious health

Reactance. Unpleasant state involving negative cognitive responses and emotions, such as counterargumentation and anger. It is the result of a perceived threat to freedom and motivates the restoration of that freedom.

Vicarious reactance. Reactance resulting from reading about, listening to, or observing threats to the freedom of others.

Boomerang effect. A situation in which the recipient's attitude or behaviour shifts in the opposite direction to that which is being advocated.

threat in response to a campaign enforcing mask-wearing behaviours), or take other liberties that give them a sense of control (see Rosenberg & Siegel, 2018; Quick et al., 2013; Steindl et al., 2015 for reviews).

8.1.1 Arousing Reactance

The level of reactance aroused depends on how important the **threatened freedom** is perceived to be, as well as the **nature of the threat**. An individual's characteristics and their propensity to react with reactance also play a role. This can be measured using scales such as the Hong Psychological Reactance Scale. However, it is debatable whether reactance can be considered a stable personality trait. For a review of reactance measurement, see Rosenberg and Siegel (2018) or Quick et al. (2013). In the context of persuasion, it is worth bearing in mind that **high-pressure communication** is likely to be perceived as a threat to freedom. This perception may arise from noticing that someone is trying to persuade us or from the manner in which they are doing so. These "how" factors include the use of intense, forceful, dogmatic, or controlling language, such as "you must admit that this is the right conclusion," "you ought to do this," and "you should evaluate it positively." Messages containing autonomy-supportive language, such as "perhaps," "possibly," and "maybe," result in less reactance than those containing such language.

Similarly, **proscriptive injunctions** (requesting that one should not do something, e.g., "you should not spend in excess of 45 hours a week on the internet") lead to greater reactance than **prescriptive injunctions** (requesting that one should do something, e.g., "you should spend less than 45 hours a week on the internet"), as the former are perceived as less legitimate (Pavey et al., 2022). Reactance can also result from the **visual components** of a persuasive message. For instance, photographs of the speaker taken from different angles can convey information about their relationship with the audience. Consequently, a low-angle shot may create a greater perceived

High-pressure communication. Communication that results in the receiver perceiving the persuasive message as threatening their freedom of choice. This could be caused by the use of intense, forceful, dogmatic, or controlling language.

Proscriptive injunctions. A request that someone should not do something.

Prescriptive injunctions. A request that someone should do something.

threat to freedom than an eye-level shot (Bünzli et al., 2025). Reactance may also result from seemingly peripheral or contextual aspects of a situation or presentation. For example, viewers may interpret the frames surrounding paintings as an attempt to influence their perception of the artwork. This can lead to reactance, causing the framed artwork to be evaluated more negatively (Koniak & Szubielska, 2022).

Restoration postscripts. Elements of the message that remind recipients of their freedom, such as "The choice is yours."

Reactance decoy. A persuasive message presented before the target message. Its purpose is to create reactance and give respondents the opportunity to express it, thus restoring their perceived freedom.

8.1.2 Reducing Reactance

Studies in communication have also focused on features of messages or situations that can reduce reactance (e.g., Rosenberg & Siegel, 2018; Quick et al., 2013; see also Section 8.3). These include **restoration postscripts**, which remind recipients of their freedom at the end of the message (e.g., "The choice is yours. You're free to decide for yourself"; Bessarabova et al., 2013). The novelty or sensational value of the message (i.e., its potential to elicit sensory, emotional, and arousal responses) may also reduce the perceived threat to freedom by shifting the recipient's attention away from the controlling aspect of the communication. Reactance can also be reduced by arousing recipients' empathy and identification with the message's characters (e.g., people describing their personal history in an anti-drug message). Furthermore, admitting at the beginning of a message that recipients might experience reactance can in fact decrease the perceived threat to freedom and increase the persuasiveness of the message. Other studies have shown that presenting a decoy message can reduce reactance. A **reactance decoy** is a persuasive message presented before the target message. Its purpose is to create reactance and give respondents the opportunity to express it by answering a question about their attitude towards the subject of the decoy message. This process restores their threatened freedom. Consequently, respondents' attitudes towards the target message increase, particularly when compared with situations in which the message presented before the target message creates less reactance than the decoy message (Schumpe et al., 2020).

8.1.3 Positive Effects of Reactance

Reactance is not just an obstacle; it can also be harnessed to achieve communication goals. To use reactance effectively as a persuasive strategy, we must provoke it in response to sources or forces advocating the opposite of what we want recipients to do, think, or feel. For instance, reading about the food industry's methods of undermining people's dietary choices can result in reactance, leading to a stronger desire to reduce meat consumption (Sprengholz & Bührig, 2025). Another example of this strategy is the anti-tobacco "Truth" campaign, which exposed the tobacco industry's marketing practices and lust for profit, highlighting their manipulation of the truth about tobacco and smoking. This campaign was more effective at increasing anti-tobacco attitudes than the "just say no" approach, which was counterproductive (Farrelly et al., 2002).

8.1.4 Reactance versus Rationalisation

It is important to note that reactance does not always occur when people are faced with restrictions or restrictive policies (e.g., prohibiting mobile phone use while driving or lowering the speed limit). In fact, it is not the default response. When faced with threats to their freedom, people often **rationalise**. Rather than opposing the restrictions and valuing the restricted option more highly, they may adapt to the given constraint and start to view it positively. The motivation to rationalise imposed restrictions stems from the tendency to **system justification**. As a result, people will not only passively accept constraints but also actively bolster the current state of affairs. This is especially likely to happen when the **restriction is absolute**, that is, when it is complete, certain, and permanent. In such situations, the only solution is to minimise the importance of the threatened freedom and adapt to the inevitable.

Reactance appears when the restriction is non-absolute, that is, when there is a chance that it will not come into effect. The restrictive policy is then evaluated negatively, and the importance of threatened freedom increases. Furthermore, reactance tends to occur when people have the cognitive capacity to recognise the restrictive nature of the policy. However, when cognitive resources are limited (due to time constraints or other disruptions) or attention is not focused on the restrictive nature of the policy, rationalisation tends to occur instead. This suggests that rationalisation and system justification are more spontaneous and implicit reactions than reactance (see Proudfoot & Kay, 2014, for a review).

Rationalisation. Adaptation to the given constraint and formation of a positive attitude towards it.

8.2 Message Position and Receiver Attitude

Negativity effect. Tendency for negative information to carry more weight than positive information in judgements and decisions.

Disconfirmation bias (also biased elaboration, biased assimilation, and biased evaluation). The tendency to evaluate arguments that are inconsistent with an individual's prior attitudes as weaker than those that are consistent with them; perception of incoming evidence as supporting one's previous attitude.

A persuasive message usually takes a consistent position on the subject of persuasion. This position may be stated more or less clearly, and the message may contain arguments and information that contradict the desired shift in the recipient's attitude, as with two-sided messages (see Section 5.3.2). Sometimes, the position is implied and must be inferred by the recipient from the structure of the argument, as with a message that omits the conclusion (see Section 5.3.2). In most cases, however, the message contains arguments about whether the object of persuasion is good or bad, depending on the persuasive goal. It also indicates whether the object should be evaluated positively or negatively (although see Section 12.3). Negative arguments tend to be more persuasive than positive ones (Cobb & Kuklinski, 1997), which is consistent with the more general tendency for negative information to carry more weight than positive information in judgements and decisions (the **negativity effect**). However, arguments and entire messages can also be encoded evaluatively – as compatible or incompatible with a person's existing attitude. Consequently, the persuasive effectiveness of pro versus con arguments can be moderated by their compatibility or incompatibility with the pre-existing attitude. Due to **disconfirmation bias** (also known as **biased elaboration**, assimilation, and evaluation; see Section 4.2), arguments that are inconsistent with attitudes are evaluated as being weaker than consistent ones, and people tend to view the overall direction of argumentation as being consistent with their pre-existing attitudes (Koniak & Cwalina, 2022).

8.2.1 Message Discrepancy

The discrepancy between the position advocated in the message and the receiver's attitude can vary in size. Two types of such discrepancy can be distinguished (Kaplowitz & Fink, 1997). The first is **positional**

Positional discrepancy. The difference between the receiver's position and the position advocated by the message when both are measured in objective units (e.g., distance, money, or time).

Psychological discrepancy. The discrepancy perceived by the receiver between the position advocated by the message and their own position.

discrepancy, which is the difference between the receiver's position and the position advocated by the message when both are measured in objective units (e.g., distance, money, or time). For instance, the persuader and the receiver may have different views on how much money should be allocated to a particular goal. The second type is **psychological discrepancy**, which is the discrepancy perceived by the receiver. This can result from positional discrepancy or from the context. For instance, preceding the focal message with a more extreme message may result in a smaller psychological discrepancy than if it were preceded by a less extreme message. Furthermore, persuasive effectiveness depends more on psychological discrepancy than positional discrepancy.

According to the **Social Judgement Theory** (Sherif & Hovland, 1961; see Eagly & Chaiken, 1993, for a review), the initial attitude of the receiver distorts their perception of the position in the persuasive message. Specifically, the receiver's own attitude serves as a reference point. The continuum along which incoming statements are evaluated can be divided into three latitudes: acceptance, noncommitment, and rejection. A statement falling within the **latitude of acceptance** (or close to it within the **latitude of noncommitment**) is **assimilated**. It is perceived as being closer to the receiver's attitude than it actually is, and the actual discrepancy between the persuader's and receiver's positions is underestimated. However, for statement falling within the **latitude of rejection** (or close to it within the latitude of noncommitment), the **contrast effect** occurs. The statement is perceived as being more distant from the receiver's attitude than it actually is, and the discrepancy between the persuader's and receiver's positions is exaggerated. The extent to which incoming statements or arguments are distorted by pre-existing attitudes depends on how much the receiver perceives the attitude as belonging to them and considers it to be part of their self-concept. The more **ego-involved** the attitude is, the more assimilation or contrast occurs. Moreover, ego-involvement affects the width of latitudes. Specifically, while it probably does not alter the breadth of the latitude of acceptance, it changes the relative sizes of the latitudes of rejection and noncommitment. As ego-involvement increases, the latitude of rejection broadens, and the latitude of noncommitment narrows or disappears completely. These processes of assimilation and contrast are particularly likely to occur in the case of ambiguous messages and/or arguments. Furthermore, factors such as the credibility of the source may widen the latitude of acceptance or narrow the latitude of rejection.

Latitude of acceptance. A range of attitudinal positions that the receiver considers acceptable.

Latitude of noncommitment. A range of attitudinal positions that the receiver considers neither acceptable nor objectionable.

Latitude of rejection. A range of attitudinal positions that the receiver rejects.

Ego-involvement. The extent to which the receiver perceives the attitude as belonging to them and considers it to be part of their self-concept.

This distorted perception of position in persuasive communication affects the extent and direction of attitude change. As long as the message is assimilated, the greater the discrepancy, the more the receiver's attitude will change in the advocated direction. However, when the message is contrasted, its persuasiveness decreases. Thus, this theory predicts an inverted U-shaped relationship between discrepancy in the message and attitude change. At more extreme levels of discrepancy, it predicts **"boomerang" attitude change**, whereby the recipient's attitude shifts in the opposite direction to that advocated.

8.2.2 The Discrepancy Motives Model

Although previous studies have generally found that counterattitudinal messages are processed more extensively than proattitudinal ones, this is not always the case. According to the Discrepancy Motives Model (Clark & Wegener, 2013), proattitudinal messages may sometimes be processed more deeply than counterattitudinal ones. The model also specifies the conditions that influence the expected outcome. According to this model, the extent to which a persuasive message is processed may be driven by two categories of motive. One category is **defence motives**, whereby people encountering a counterattitudinal message may be motivated to defend their initial attitude against this perceived attack. This is

Defence motives. Motivation to defend initial attitude against perceived attack.

because such a message implies that the recipient's attitude is incorrect, which threatens people's desire to hold correct attitudes. In this situation, people process the message more extensively in order to reject it. However, people can also be driven by **bolstering motives**. They may seek support for their existing attitudes in order to strengthen them. Studies on selective exposure (see Sections 4.1 and 12.3) show that people prefer to read or hear information that is consistent with their existing attitudes because they wish to avoid the negative state associated with cognitive dissonance (see Sections 4.1 and 5.4). Bolstering motivation may be satisfied not only by avoiding information that contradicts one's attitude but also by thoroughly processing information that confirms its accuracy.

Bolstering motives. Motivation to support existing attitudes in order to strengthen them.

Whether defence or bolstering motives prevail is determined by the properties of pre-existing attitudes and the persuasive communication properties, such as the characteristics of the message senders. The interaction between these persuasion variables and the position advocated in the message determines the likelihood of message processing. Overall, when pre-message attitudes are strong (i.e., low ambivalence scores, high accessibility scores, or high certainty scores), defence motivation prevails, enhancing the processing of counterattitudinal rather than proattitudinal messages. Conversely, when initial attitudes are weak (i.e., high ambivalence scores, low accessibility scores, or low certainty scores), bolstering motivation increases and proattitudinal messages are processed more extensively than counterattitudinal ones.

The source of the message may also influence which motivation will prevail, depending on whether it takes a pro- or counterattitudinal position. When a credible or efficacious source takes a counterattitudinal position, people are motivated to defend their pre-existing attitudes. Counterattitudinal messages from a credible or efficacious source are processed more extensively than those from an inefficient or uncredible source, as the latter are not perceived as threatening. Conversely, proattitudinal messages from an inefficient or uncredible source motivate attitude bolstering. In such situations, recipients favour the advocacy but are concerned that it may be unsuccessful due to the possibility of flawed or ineffective argumentation. This results in enhanced processing of proattitudinal messages from sources seen as low in credibility or efficiency. When a credible or efficient source takes a position that aligns with that favoured by the recipient, there is no cause for concern, so such messages are not extensively processed.

8.3 Approach-Avoidance Model of Persuasion

Attitude objects, offers, messages, advertisements and requests, are often complex stimuli that engage two classes of motives. The first class of motives is **approach motives**, which push opinions and behaviours towards the goal. The other class of motives is **avoidance motives**, which push opinions and behaviours away from the goal. For example, when the government tries to persuade people to buy electric cars, individuals may be attracted by economic incentives, lower running costs, or the environmentally friendly image of electric vehicles. However, they may also be deterred by the higher initial cost, limited range, and the perceived inconvenience of charging.

> **Approach motives**. The motives or forces that push opinions and behaviours towards the goal.
>
> **Avoidance motives**. The motives or forces that push opinions and behaviours away from the goal.
>
> **Alpha strategies**. Persuasion strategies that focus on increasing approach motivation.
>
> **Omega strategies**. Persuasion strategies that focus on decreasing avoidance motivation.

According to the approach-avoidance model of persuasion (Knowles & Linn, 2004; Knowles & Riner, 2007), the effectiveness of persuasion depends on the **ratio of approach and avoidance forces**. When approach motives are stronger, people move towards the goal. However, when avoidance motives are stronger, people will move in the opposite direction to that which they are being persuaded. Therefore, to persuade people to do something, one can either increase approach forces or decrease avoidance forces. Persuasion strategies that focus on increasing approach motivation are called **Alpha strategies**, while those that focus on decreasing avoidance motivation are called **Omega strategies**.

8.3.1 Alpha Strategies for Persuasion

The strategies in this group either increase people's desire for the object of persuasion or create it if it did not previously exist. One obvious approach is to **make the message more persuasive**, for example, by strengthening the argumentation or tailoring it to the intended recipient (see Section 12.1). Other Alpha strategies are mostly based on the principles and techniques described by Cialdini (2021). These include offering **incentives**, such as bonuses for purchasing the promoted goods, or implying that adopting a particular opinion will earn respect. Increasing the perceived **credibility or attractiveness** of the source can also make the opinion or offer more appealing. Similarly, providing information about social consensus (**social proof**) – information indicating that others evaluate something positively – can increase people's preference for a particular option. Emphasising the **scarcity** of an object can increase its appeal, as this implies popularity and can serve as social proof. However, it can also induce competitiveness. As a result, it may burden the decision-making process and reduce resistance, meaning this mechanism can be also considered an example of an Omega strategy. Examples of Alpha strategies also include engaging the norm of **reciprocity**. When someone is done a favour, they feel obligated to reciprocate, which may be fulfilled by accepting a persuasive suggestion. Another strategy is based on emphasising **consistency and commitment**. Committing the receiver to an opinion can make them more likely to comply with extreme persuasive messages that align with their previously expressed views.

8.3.2 *Omega Strategies for Persuasion*

The strategies in this group can be classified into seven subgroups, each containing various specific strategies. Here, we will discuss some examples, including those not presented by Knowles and Linn (2004). The first group of Omega strategies is based on the principle of **sidestepping resistance** to prevent it from arising in the first place. This can be achieved by **redefining the relationship** between the receiver and the persuader. For instance, a salesperson might refer to themselves as a consultant. The idea is to eliminate any suggestion that the relationship is asymmetrical or that persuasion is taking place. Using an **anthropomorphised messenger** ("talking" products, e.g.) instead of a human messenger can have a similar effect. While this does not make persuasion more effective for people with high interpersonal trust, it is significantly more effective for those with low trust. Therefore, for individuals with low interpersonal trust, an anthropomorphised messenger could help to avoid arousing suspicion (Touré-Tillery & McGill, 2015). Similarly, messages from comedians may discourage counterargument and encourage consideration of arguments. However, such **humorous messages** may be dismissed as irrelevant during the decision-making process. Nevertheless, due to the sleeper effect (see Section 5.1), these messages may become more persuasive over time (Nabi et al., 2007). Another strategy aimed at circumventing resistance involves **attacking values in order to indirectly change attitudes**. People are relatively good at resisting direct attacks on their attitudes because they are often discussed and challenged. However, the values related to these attitudes are rarely discussed or challenged, and are some form of cultural truisms. Therefore, attacking values related to an attitude may be a more effective form of persuasion than attacking the attitude directly. Blankenship and colleagues (2012) demonstrated this idea in a study in which they showed that the same persuasive message changed attitudes towards affirmative action more when it was presented as an attack on the value of equality than when it was presented as an attack on affirmative action itself.

The second group comprises strategies that are designed to **directly address the resistance** expected to arise from a persuasive attempt. One example is including negative information in **two-sided messages** (see Section 5.3.2 and Section 12.3.2), which counters potential objections from the audience. Furthermore, even when messages are framed as two-sided but do not contain any negative information about the object of persuasion, they reduce the audience's willingness to consider this object's flaws. This occurs among receivers with a high need for cognition, who, in the case of a one-sided message, consider possible negatives (Rucker et al., 2008). Therefore, simply framing a message as two-sided can help to cancel out the otherwise aroused resistance.

Third, expected resistance can be **indirectly addressed by eliminating the need for a resistant reaction**. This can be achieved by raising the self-esteem of the person receiving the message. According to **self-affirmation theory** (Sherman & Cohen, 2006), defensive responses (including resistance to persuasion) result from people's motivation to protect their sense of self-integrity. However, when faced with threats to their self-integrity, people may engage in indirect psychological adaptations. They may affirm alternative self-resources, even those unrelated to the threat. For example, people may affirm their sense of self by reflecting on important aspects of their life or by engaging in activities that highlight important values, even if these are irrelevant to the threat. These activities serve as a reminder of who they are. Consequently, the impact of the threatening event (e.g., a persuasive message) on self-integrity is reduced. For instance, Sherman and collaborators (2000) showed a video about AIDS-related risk to sexually active participants. Those who had previously engaged in self-affirmation (by writing about their most important value) perceived themselves as being at a greater risk of contracting HIV. Consequently, they purchased condoms more frequently than those who had not engaged in self-affirmation.

Fourth, resistance can be **distracted** (see Section 7.1.1). Fifth, it may be **disrupted**. For example, any element of a persuasive situation that confuses the recipient may draw their critical attention, resulting in uncertainty and increased openness to persuasive suggestions. Sixth, as resistance is a motivational process, it can be **depleted**. For instance, people evaluated a political candidate more positively when they saw an advertisement advocating for this candidate first, rather than when the advertisement was presented after six other political advertisements had been evaluated. However, this only worked for people who were not very sceptical, that is, those with little resistance or experience of using their resistance resources. For those who are more sceptical and skilled at resistance, the effect may be reversed, with each subsequent advertisement mobilising their greater reactance resources (Knowles & Linn, 2004; Knowles & Riner, 2007). Finally, **resistance can be used against itself**. We will discuss one example of this strategy, namely paradoxical thinking, in more detail in Section 11.4.3.

Further Readings

Knowles, E. S., & Linn, J. A. (Eds.). (2004). *Resistance and persuasion*. Hillsdale, NJ: Lawrence Erlbaum Associates.

Sherman, D. K., & Cohen, G. L. (2006). The psychology of self-defense: Self-affirmation theory. In M. P. Zanna (Ed.), *Advances in experimental social psychology* (Vol. 38, pp. 183–242). New York: Academic Press.

References

Bessarabova, E., Fink, E. L., & Turner, M. (2013). Reactance, restoration, and cognitive structure: Comparative statics. *Human Communication Research, 39*, 339–364.

Blankenship, K. L., Wegener, D. T., & Murray, R. A. (2012). Circumventing resistance: Using values to indirectly change attitudes. *Journal of Personality and Social Psychology, 103*(4), 606–621.

Brehm, J. W. (1966). *A theory of psychological reactance*. New York: Academic Press.

Brehm, S. S., & Brehm, J. W. (1981). *Psychological reactance: A theory of freedom and control*. New York: Academic Press.

Bünzli, F., Dillard, J. P., Li, Y., & Eppler, M. J. (2025). When visual communication backfires: Reactance to three aspects of imagery. *Communication Research, 52*(5), 683–713.

Cialdini, R. B. (2021). *Influence: The psychology of persuasion*. New York: HarperCollins.

Clark, J. K., & Wegener, D. T. (2013). Message position, information processing, and persuasion: The discrepancy motives model. *Advances in Experimental Social Psychology, 47*, 189–232.

Cobb, M. D., & Kuklinski, J. H. (1997). Changing minds: Political arguments and political persuasion. *American Journal of Political Science, 41*(1), 88–121.

Dillard, J. P., & Shen, L. (2005). On the nature of reactance and its role in persuasive health communication. *Communication Monographs, 72*(2), 144–168.

Eagly, A. H., & Chaiken, S. (1993). *The psychology of attitudes*. Harcourt Brace Jovanovich College Publishers.

Farrelly, M. C., Healton, C. G., Davis, K. C., Messeri, P., Hersey, J. C., & Haviland, M. L. (2002). Getting to the truth: Evaluating national tobacco countermarketing campaigns. *American Journal of Public Health*, *92*(6), 901–907.

Kaplowitz, S. A., & Fink, E. L. (1997). Message discrepancy and persuasion. In G. A. Barnett, & F. J. Boster (Eds.), *Progress in communication sciences* (Vol. 13, pp. 75–106). Norwood, NJ: Ablex.

Knowles, E. S., & Linn, J. A. (2004). Approach-avoidance model of persuasion: Alpha and omega strategies for change. In E. S. Knowles, & J. A. Linn (Eds.), *Resistance and persuasion* (pp. 117–148). Hillsdale, NJ: Lawrence Erlbaum Associates.

Knowles, E. S., & Riner, D. D. (2007). Omega approaches to persuasion: Overcoming resistance. In A. R. Pratkanis (Ed.), *The science of social influence: Advances and future progress* (pp. 83–114). New York: Psychology Press.

Koniak, P., & Cwalina, W. (2022). Forbid/allow asymmetry in persuasion: The forbid frame decreases biased elaboration and increases attitude change. *Social Psychology*, *53*(1), 1–20.

Koniak, P., & Szubielska, M. (2022). On the peripheries of contemporary paintings: Impact of frame decorativeness on the reception of abstract artwork. *Annals of Psychology*, *25*(2), 121–136.

Nabi, R. L., Moyer-Gusé, E., & Byrne, S. (2007). All joking aside: A serious investigation into the persuasive effect of funny social issue messages. *Communication Monographs*, *74*(1), 29–54.

Pavey, L., Churchill, S., & Sparks, P. (2022). Proscriptive injunctions can elicit greater reactance and lower legitimacy perceptions than prescriptive injunctions. *Personality and Social Psychology Bulletin*, *48*(5), 676–689.

Proudfoot, D., & Kay, A. C. (2014). Reactance or rationalization? Predicting public responses to government policy. *Policy Insights from the Behavioral and Brain Sciences*, *1*(1), 256–262.

Quick, B. L., Shen, L., & Dillard, J. P. (2013). Reactance theory and persuasion. In J. P. Dillard, & L. Shen (Eds.), *The Sage handbook of persuasion: Developments in theory and practice* (2nd ed., pp. 167–183). Thousand Oaks, CA: Sage Publications.

Rosenberg, B. D., & Siegel, J. T. (2018). A 50-year review of psychological reactance theory: Do not read this article. *Motivation Science*, *4*(4), 281–300.

Rucker, D. D., Petty, R. E., & Briñol, P. (2008). What's in a frame anyway?: A meta-cognitive analysis of the impact of one versus two sided message framing on attitude certainty. *Journal of Consumer Psychology*, *18*(2), 137–149.

Schumpe, B. M., Bélanger, J. J., & Nisa, C. F. (2020). The reactance decoy effect: How including an appeal before a target message increases persuasion. *Journal of Personality and Social Psychology*, *119*(2), 272–292.

Sherif, M., & Hovland, C. I. (1961). *Social judgment: Assimilation and contrast effects in communication and attitude change.* New Haven, CT: Yale University Press.

Sherman, D. K., & Cohen, G. L. (2006). The psychology of self-defense: Self-affirmation theory. In M. P. Zanna (Ed.), *Advances in experimental social psychology* (Vol. 38, pp. 183–242). New York: Academic Press.

Sherman, D. A. K., Nelson, L. D., & Steele, C. M. (2000). Do messages about health risks threaten the self? Increasing the acceptance of threatening health messages via self-affirmation. *Personality and Social Psychology Bulletin, 26*(9), 1046–1058.

Sprengholz, P., & Bührig, D. (2025). Reactance as a persuasive strategy: How health communication can harness anger to leverage behavior change. *Health Communication, 40*(11), 2200–2206.

Steindl, C., Jonas, E., Sittenthaler, S., Traut-Mattausch, E., & Greenberg, J. (2015). Understanding psychological reactance: New developments and findings. *Zeitschrift für Psychologie, 223*(4), 205–214.

Touré-Tillery, M., & McGill, A. L. (2015). Who or what to believe: Trust and the differential persuasiveness of human and anthropomorphized messengers. *Journal of Marketing, 79*(4), 94–110.

Chapter 9

Narrative Persuasion

Most studies of persuasion focus on changing attitudes through rhetoric and argumentation. However, various narratives can also influence how people perceive the world, as well as their thoughts and feelings. The persuasive power of novels, films, stories, TV series, soap operas, video games, and other forms of storytelling has long been recognised by various authorities, as evidenced by their attempts at censorship. Propagandists recognised this, too. For instance, films played a significant role in Nazi propaganda, fostering negative perceptions of foreign nations deemed enemies of the regime and inciting hatred towards Jews, while cultivating favourable attitudes towards the National Socialist movement and Hitler (Weinberg, 1984). Intelligence services also employed narratives. For example, the CIA printed copies of Boris Pasternak's novel *Doctor Zhivago* and smuggled them into the Soviet Union. This was because they viewed the novel's message as a potential threat to the communist system (Finn & Couvée, 2014). Overall, people spent more time watching and reading narrative stories than materials based on rhetorical argumentation, such as current affairs programmes or editorials. Furthermore, narratives have become ubiquitous, appearing not only in materials created for entertainment purposes but also in other contexts. Advertisements, which aim to persuade, often take the form of a narrative (Brechman & Purvis, 2015).

The persuasive power of narrative stories has been observed in a variety of contexts. Reading the *Harry Potter* books has been linked to more positive attitudes towards marginalised groups (Muslims and homosexuals), less support for punitive policies (such as torture to extract information, killing terrorists, and the death penalty), and lower approval ratings for Donald Trump. However, watching the *Harry Potter* films has only been found to be related to attitudes towards some of these issues (Mutz, 2016). Studies have shown that exposure to dystopian narratives, such as *The Hunger Games* and *Divergent*, leads to a greater justification of radical political action and more positive attitudes towards violent protests. Furthermore, dystopian fiction has a greater impact on attitudes than

DOI: 10.4324/9781003589174-11

news reports about real-life protests against autocratic and unjust regimes (Jones & Paris, 2018). Diekman and her colleagues (2000) found that women who read a lot of romance novels had a more negative view of condom use. This was probably because romance novels rarely depict condom use during initial sexual encounters. However, one of their experiments found that participants' attitudes towards condoms became more positive when they read romance stories that included elements of safe sex. Overall, narrative messages have been shown to be more persuasive than non-narrative ones in terms of both immediate and delayed measures of effectiveness (Oschatz & Marker, 2020).

9.1 Transportation Theory

According to Green and Brock (2000, 2005), the persuasiveness of a narrative depends on a process known as **transportation**. They describe this as "a distinct mental process, an integrative melding of attention, imagery, and feelings" (Green & Brock, 2000, p. 701). It is an experience in which all mental systems and capacities focus on the narrative. Consequently, the reader, viewer, listener, or player becomes somewhat disconnected from the real world and loses access to real-world facts. However, while in this state, they accept the reality of the narrative world in which they are immersed. Consequently, they pay little attention to the relationship between the facts and assertions in the narrative and the facts of the real world. Furthermore, this state evokes strong emotions and motivations that the person experiencing it feels even when they know the world depicted in the narrative is not real. Finally, when people finish reading or viewing and return to the real world, they are changed to some extent, and this change may be reflected in their beliefs and attitudes.

Green and Brock (2000) tested their predictions by presenting participants with various stories taken from anthologies, popular magazines, and best-selling non-fiction books. One of these stories was about a young girl who was brutally murdered in a shopping centre by a psychiatric patient. They found that the level of transportation was associated with a change in beliefs consistent with the story. Participants who were highly transported by the story of the murder in the shopping centre were more likely to believe that violence is more commonplace, that the world is less just, and that crime is more prevalent. They were also more willing to restrict the freedom of psychiatric patients. Thus, transportation not

Transportation. A distinct mental process that occurs in a person engaged in a narrative, and it is an integrative melding of attention, imagery, and feelings.

only led to the formation of beliefs related to the story itself but also to beliefs implied by the narrative. Overall, experiencing transportation enhances the persuasive impact of narrative stories on readers' beliefs and attitudes.

Transportability. The individual's ability to be transported.

Need for affect. The motivation to approach (or avoid) situations and activities that evoke emotions.

The level of transportation depends on many factors. First, it depends on the characteristics of the reader (or viewer, etc.). People differ in their ability to be transported, that is, their **transportability**. These relatively stable individual differences can be measured using the **Transportability Scale** (Dal Cin et al., 2004). The extent to which a person is transported into the story world is also determined by their **need for affect** (Appel & Richter, 2010), which is defined as "general motivation of people to approach or avoid situations and activities that are emotion inducing" (Maio & Esses, 2001, p. 585). Furthermore, prior familiarity with the story's theme, as well as pre-existing tendencies to sympathise with the story's characters (e.g., having a friend in the same social group as the character), can increase transportation (Green, 2004). Another scale, the Transportation Scale, is used to measure transportation resulting from a specific narrative at a specific time (Green & Brock, 2000). Thus, transportation is also a function of the quality of the story, whether it is a text or film, for example. Labelling a story as fictional or factual does not affect the level of transportation. Finally, the widely defined context may also affect the level of transportation. For example, whether the narrative is self-paced or externally paced (Moyer-Gusé & Dale, 2017).

Transportation differs from the cognitive elaboration described by dual-process models of persuasion (see Chapter 7). It reduces negative cognitive responses and counterargumentation. Those who are transported do not counterargue the claims of a story, as this would disrupt their immersion in it and the positive feelings associated with it. Furthermore, stories are generally presented as entertainment rather than as persuasive acts, so they do not elicit resistance (and may be considered examples of omega strategies of persuasion – see Dal Cin et al., 2004, and Section 8.3). Escalas (2007) demonstrated that the benefits of transportation can also be obtained through advertisements. Participants who read an advertisement inducing **analytical self-referencing** ("We'd like to introduce you to Westerly running shoes, designed with you in mind") evaluated the brand positively when the arguments were strong and negatively when they were weak. However, the attitudes of participants who read an advertisement inducing **narrative self-referencing** ("Imagine yourself running through this park… Westerly running shoes on your feet") were unaffected by the quality of the argumentation. Their attitudes were as positive as those of participants who read the advertisement with analytical self-referencing and strong argumentation. Furthermore, participants in the narrative self-referencing group generated fewer counterarguments than those in the analytical self-referencing group.

Analytical self-referencing. Cognitive elaboration based on analysing incoming information by relating them to one's self or one's personal experiences.

Narrative self-referencing. A process based on transportation, where people become absorbed in their story like thoughts.

Furthermore, Slater and colleagues (2006) found that television drama narratives can influence public opinion on controversial policies such as the death penalty. Support for the death penalty increased among viewers who watched an episode of a crime drama featuring the brutal murder of a woman, followed by an investigation and trial. Moreover, the death penalty attitudes of participants from control group were predicted by their ideology (degree of liberalism/conservatism). However, watching the crime drama episode weakened this relationship, reducing it to non-significant levels. This suggests that narratives can suppress the effects of ideology on attitudes.

Narratives may also cause people to accept **false information** as truth. Gerrig and Prentice (1991) demonstrated that readers integrate information obtained from fiction into their existing knowledge of the real world, even when this information contradicts reality ("mental illness is contagious", e.g.). This can subsequently influence their judgements in the real world. Appel and Richter (2007) found that people more agree with false statements expressing everyday beliefs (such as "exercise weakens your heart and lungs") when they are presented with a fictional narrative conveying this false information. Moreover, this effect does not fade over time but rather increases (the "sleeper effect"; see Section 5.1). Furthermore, although the certainty of these false beliefs was weakened immediately after reading false information, after two weeks, this certainty returned to baseline levels. Therefore, belief in false information read in a fictional narrative became stronger over time, and participants became more certain that these beliefs were true.

Further Reading

Green, M. C., & Appel, M. (2024). Narrative transportation: How stories shape how we see ourselves and the world. *Advances in Experimental Social Psychology, 70*, 1–82.

References

Appel, M., & Richter, T. (2007). Persuasive effects of fictional narratives increase over time. *Media Psychology, 10*(1), 113–134.

Appel, M., & Richter, T. (2010). Transportation and need for affect in narrative persuasion: A mediated moderation model. *Media Psychology, 13*(2), 101–135.

Brechman, J. M., & Purvis, S. C. (2015). Narrative, transportation and advertising. *International Journal of Advertising, 34*(2), 366–381.

Dal Cin, S., Zanna, M. P., & Fong, G. T. (2004). Narrative persuasion and overcoming resistance. In E. S. Knowles, & J. A. Linn (Eds.), *Resistance and persuasion* (pp. 175–191). Hillsdale, NJ: Lawrence Erlbaum Associates.

Diekman, A. B., McDonald, M., & Gardner, W. L. (2000). Love means never having to be careful: The relationship between reading romance novels and safe sex behavior. *Psychology of Women Quarterly, 24*(2), 179–188.

Escalas, J. E. (2007). Self-referencing and persuasion: Narrative transportation versus analytical elaboration. *Journal of Consumer Research, 33*(4), 421–429.

Finn, P., & Couvée, P. (2014). *The Zhivago Affair: The Kremlin, the CIA, and the battle over a forbidden book*. New York: Pantheon Books.

Gerrig, R. J., & Prentice, D. A. (1991). The representation of fictional information. *Psychological Science, 2*(5), 336–340.

Green, M. C. (2004). Transportation into narrative worlds: The role of prior knowledge and perceived realism. *Discourse Processes, 38*(2), 247–266.

Green, M. C., & Brock, T. C. (2000). The role of transportation in the persuasiveness of public narratives. *Journal of Personality and Social Psychology, 79*(5), 701–721.

Green, M. C., & Brock, T. C. (2005). Persuasiveness of narratives. In T. C. Brock, & M. C. Green (Eds.), *Persuasion: Psychological insights and perspectives* (2nd ed., pp. 117–142). Thousand Oaks, CA: Sage Publications.

Jones, C. W., & Paris, C. (2018). It's the end of the world and they know it: How dystopian fiction shapes political attitudes. *Perspectives on Politics, 16*(4), 969–989.

Maio, G. R., & Esses, V. M. (2001). The need for affect: Individual differences in the motivation to approach or avoid emotions. *Journal of Personality, 69*(4), 583–615.

Moyer-Gusé, E., & Dale, K. (2017). Narrative persuasion theories. In P. Rössler, C. A. Hoffner, & L. Zoonen (Eds.), *The international encyclopedia of media effects* (pp. 1–11). New York: John Wiley & Sons.

Mutz, D. C. (2016). Harry Potter and the Deathly Donald. *PS: Political Science & Politics, 49*(4), 722–729.

Oschatz, C., & Marker, C. (2020). Long-term persuasive effects in narrative communication research: A meta-analysis. *Journal of Communication, 70*(4), 473–496.

Slater, M. D., Rounder, D., & Long, M. (2006). Television dramas and support for controversial public policies: Effects and mechanisms. *Journal of Communication, 56*(2), 235–252.

Weinberg, D. (1984). Approaches to the study of film in the Third Reich: A critical appraisal. *Journal of Contemporary History, 19*(1), 105–126.

Part 3

Key Methodologies

This section in summary

- Self-report attitude measurements: single-item and multi-item scales
- Measurements of implicit attitudes
- Physiological measurements of attitude
- Brain imaging-based attitude measurements

DOI: 10.4324/9781003589174-12

Chapter 10

Measuring Attitudes

Scientists studying attitudes in social psychology and other fields (e.g., political science, sociology, or marketing) strive not only to theoretically describe and understand attitudes. The starting point of any scientific endeavour is observation and measurement. Therefore, we must know what to look for and how to express it numerically. Measuring attitudes is necessary to predict human behaviour. This is based on the assumption that if we know people's attitudes, we will know why and how they react to various objects. This is complemented by gaining knowledge about whether and how attitudes change under the influence of persuasion. Such understanding is necessary to influence people (e.g., through advertising or face-to-face interactions) and to equip them with tools to defend themselves against such influence. Therefore, attitude measurement has both theoretical and practical dimensions.

Many different methods of measuring attitudes have been developed. The first group of methods involves directly asking people about their attitudes towards a given object (*direct self-report measures*). An alternative and complementary approach is *indirect measurement techniques*, which aim to overcome the problem of intentional and unintentional distortions when reporting one's own attitudes directly. A detailed description of attitude measurement methods, the assumptions on which they are based, and their advantages and disadvantages can be found in Krosnick et al. (2019).

10.1 Single-Item Direct Measurement

The simplest way to measure attitudes is to ask people a single direct question to describe their attitudes. This measurement method is also referred to as survey-type, as it is commonly used in surveys. However, it can also be found in marketing research and scientific articles.

Such a direct question can take various forms. It can be asked directly, with a scale specifying the responses. For example, "Are you a supporter or opponent of alternative medicine?" where responses are on a scale

DOI: 10.4324/9781003589174-13

of points (usually 5 or 7 points) ranging from "strongly opposed" to "strongly supported." A single item can also be expressed as a statement (positive or negative), for example, "Do you agree with the statement that alternative medicine (isn't) an effective treatment?" In this case, responses are also on a scale, this time from "strongly disagree" to "strongly agree."

A **feeling thermometer** scale is also used to measure attitudes. Respondents are asked to express their overall attitude towards a given item. In its basic form, the "thermometer" is a line (in the online version, it's a slider), on which the respondent marks the point that best reflects their feelings. This line is described by three numbers: "0" at the left end, meaning the respondent dislikes the item; "50" in the middle, indicating a neutral attitude; and "100" at the right end, which corresponds to the maximum liking of the object. This method of measuring attitudes is usually used in studies to assess attitudes towards political candidates (see Cwalina et al., 2015).

A similar approach to the feeling thermometer is the pictorial measurement. In this case, the respondent's task is to select a pictographically depicted face with a specific expression (from a grimace to a full smile) that best reflects their evaluation of the object.

The main advantage of single-item direct measurement is its simplicity. However, such a single-question measurement also has many drawbacks. These drawbacks relate to various factors that influence the distortion of attitude reporting. These may concern the structural features of the measurement method and individual items contained within it: the positioning of the question within the survey (*question order effect*), the order in which the answer options are presented (e.g., from negative to positive or vice versa; *response order effect*), the specification of all or some of the alternatives (*question balance effect*), whether a "middle" answer can be given (e.g., "no opinion" or "neither for nor against"; *middle alternative effect*), or the tone of the question (*tone of wording effect*). One of the most frequently analysed manifestations of this effect is the forbid/allow asymmetry (Koniak & Cwalina, 2022). For example, in a classic study, Rugg (1941) showed that if the question concerned allowing public speeches against democracy, 75% of the respondents chose an answer indicating that they were against such speeches (i.e., they answered the speeches should not be allowed). However, if the question concerned bidding public speeches against democracy, only 54% of the respondents were against such speeches (i.e., they answered they supported the ban).

In addition to biases in attitude reporting related to the structure of the measurement method, individual factors also influence attitudes, such as social desirability (providing answers that are socially acceptable) or choosing middle options, especially when questions concern sensitive or controversial issues (see Krosnick et al., 2019).

Such biases, whether intentional or not, apply to all attitude measurement methods based on self-report, but they particularly affect single-item measures. Detailed discussions of factors influencing response behaviour and ways to prevent them can be found, for example, in Krosnick (1999) and Schuman and Presser (1981).

10.2 Multi-Item Direct Measures

Because any single-item measure can contain hidden bias and ambiguity in word choice and response types, researchers tend to favour multi-item measures, which, at least to some extent, mitigate this problem. Moreover, even a single-item measure free from bias and ambiguity is often insufficient to fully capture attitudes.

10.2.1 Thurstone's Equal-Appearing Intervals Method

The equal-appearing intervals method, developed by Thurstone (1928), is a classic and still one of the best ways to measure attitudes. This method consists of several steps. The first step is to collect and generate a significant number (usually around 100) of statements containing favourable and unfavourable evaluations of a given object (e.g., alternative medicine). These statements are then reviewed to eliminate duplicates and ambiguities. In the next step, judges evaluate all remaining statements, placing them into 11 separate piles. These piles represent a continuum divided into equal intervals, the ends of which represent an extremely negative and extremely positive evaluation of a given object. In the next step, each statement is assigned a numerical value (from 1 to 11) corresponding to its location, and the mean and variance for the statement are calculated based on the ratings of all judges. Statements characterised by high variance (and therefore rated differently by different individuals) are eliminated from further scale construction. Next, two or three statements are selected whose meaning is closest to a given point on the continuum. This procedure results in a battery of items, equally spaced from one to another. The respondent's task is to select from this set those statements with which they agree. The result is the mean scale value of the statements they endorse.

10.2.2 Likert's Method of Summated Ratings

The method of summated ratings was developed by Likert (1932), in part as a measure of attitudes that is easier and less labour-intensive than Thurstone's proposal. The first step, however, is similar: collecting evaluative statements (positive and negative) that describe the attitude object.

This set is then pretested. Respondents (or judges) respond to each statement by selecting one of the response options. The standard five options are strongly approve, approve, undecided, disapprove, or strongly disapprove. Responses are assigned a point value, with higher scores corresponding to more positive evaluations. A total score is then calculated for each respondent, consisting of the sum of the scores from all items. Finally, correlations between this partial score and the total score are calculated for each item and for all individuals. The final method typically includes items with the strongest correlations. This scale is used in research, and each respondent indicates the degree to which they agree or disagree with each statement.

10.2.3 Semantic Differential

The semantic differential is a relatively simple and widely used method of measuring attitudes, developed by Osgood et al. (1957). Unlike the methods developed by Thurstone and Likert, which are issue-specific, the semantic differential can be used to measure attitudes towards a wide variety of objects. The differential typically consists of several or more bipolar scales. These are generally seven-point scales. Highly evaluative adjectives with opposite meanings describe the extremes (e.g., good/bad, positive/negative, smart/stupid). Respondents rate the object or concept (e.g., "Indicate the extent to which alternative medicine is, in your opinion...") on each of these bipolar scales. An attitude score for each item is typically calculated by assigning a value of 7 to the most positive rating, a value of 6 to a slightly less positive rating, and so on. The overall score is calculated by summing or averaging the ratings across all items. It is worth noting that in Osgood et al.'s (1957) original conceptualisation and research, the pairs of adjectives they selected described three dimensions of object perception: evaluation, potency, and activity.

The advantage of this method is that the pairs of adjectives in the semantic differential are usually general properties that can apply to virtually any topic, whether a person or an abstract concept (e.g., democracy).

10.3 Open-Ended Questions

In addition to using measurement scales, attitudes are also inferred from respondents' responses to open-ended questions. This allows individuals to describe their attitudes in their own words and express their thoughts as they wish (e.g., "Tell me, what do you think about alternative medicine?"). The main advantage of such a measure is that it does not limit people's responses. This allows them to provide rich data, such as comments about the reasons for holding a particular attitude and information reflecting subtle differences in how an issue is interpreted. This makes open-ended questions particularly useful during the initial stages of analysing a specific issue. However, the interpretation of the obtained results, as well as the effort and time required to analyse the collected responses, poses a challenge.

One solution to this problem is to ask individuals to introspect separately each aspect of their attitudes, which they mentioned in their response, and compile lists of specific beliefs, and emotions. Participants then assign a valence to each item on the lists. This can be used to calculate an index and numerically express the overall attitude towards a given object. This procedure was used in studies by, for example, Crites et al. (1994).

10.3.1 The Evaluative Lexicon (EL)

The EL is a procedure developed by Rocklage and Fazio (2015). It represents a significant modification and simplification of the procedure developed by Crites et al. (1994). The EL assumes that people's attitudes towards various objects can be measured by analysing the language they use to describe them, and more specifically, the adjectives they use. The EL consists of a list of 94 adjectives that people use in their statements to describe their evaluation of a given object. This list was developed based on preliminary research in which judges rated a set of selected adjectives on 9-point scales based on their valence (negativity–positivity) and the emotionality they imply. Consequently, each adjective has two basic, normative values, established on the basis of these analyses. Attitude measurement involves participants selecting those adjectives that describe their evaluation of a given object (e.g., alternative medicine or a specific product), and from among them, those that best describe this evaluation. The attitude index is the sum (or average) of the normative values of the selected adjectives. The EL was developed for the specific purpose of measuring attitudes, and therefore differs from other text analysis systems, such as the Linguistic Inquiry and Word Count (LIWC; Pennebaker et al., 2007), which analyses positive and negative emotion words that people write. Rocklage and Fazio (2015, p. 219) emphasise that "If researchers aim to measure individuals' attitudes towards a given object, this can be done by asking participants to select adjectives from a predefined list and then using the normative ratings associated with these adjectives in order to assess the attitudes and their bases."

10.4 Indirect Measurement Techniques

The main limitation of direct self-report measures is that they provide valid and reliable measures of attitudes only when people are willing to answer questions accurately and honestly. However, many factors prevent this from happening. These include motivational factors (e.g., a desire for a positive self-presentation), ability factors (e.g., not understanding the question), and limited access to one's own introspection regarding mental and affective processes (see Nisbett & Wilson, 1977). Due to these limitations, researchers have developed a number of indirect measurement techniques that attempt to overcome the problem of intentional and unintentional biases in attitude measurement. Most of these methods rely on measuring reaction time as a manifestation of attitude activation and associations related to the target.

10.4.1 Evaluative Priming Task (EPT)

The main idea of the evaluative priming task (EPT) is that if the activated attitude towards an object is positive, it speeds up judgements about other objects towards which we hold positive attitudes and slows down judgements about objects towards which we hold negative attitudes. The same applies if the spontaneously elicited attitude is negative (Fazio et al., 1986).

Evaluative priming procedures involve presenting participants with a double-judgement task in which they are told to first see a first priming word on a computer screen (e.g., "alternative medicine"), which they are asked to memorise, and then see a second target word (e.g., "good" or "bad"), about which they must make a value judgement (i.e., judge whether the word is positive or negative). Respondents are presented with pairs of words, and the time it takes them to make a judgement about the second word in the pair is recorded by a computer. If a person's attitude towards alternative medicine is positive, then making a judgement about the second word when "alternative medicine" precedes positive terms should be faster than when it precedes negative words. If, on the contrary, attitudes towards alternative medicine are negative, then making a judgement about the second word when "alternative medicine" precedes negative words should be faster than when it precedes positive words.

10.4.2 Implicit Association Test (IAT)

The IAT, developed by Greenwald et al. (1998), is the most commonly used indirect measure of attitudes, both in psychological research and in the fields of electoral and political behaviour and organisational science.

The IAT is a computer-based measurement based on reaction times. The test relies on categorisation tasks involving stimuli: words (e.g., alternative medicine, doctor, or shaman) or pictures (e.g., a photo of a doctor, a healer). The participant's task is to assign the stimulus to four different categories: two contrasting categories specific to the study (e.g., alternative medicine and conventional medicine) and two word categories reflecting either evaluative judgements (e.g., good/bad; pleasant/unpleasant) or descriptive judgements (e.g., self/other). A stimulus (e.g., the term "alternative medicine") appears in the centre of the computer screen, and the participant is asked to quickly assign it to one of two groups (appearing as labels on the right and left sides of the screen). These labels represent either a test-specific category (e.g., "health") or a word category (e.g., "pleasant"). The participant assigns the stimulus by pressing a key on the left side of the keyboard (to assign the stimulus to the category on the left label) or on the right side of the keyboard (to select the category on the right label). After completing the simple two-category categorisation task, the participant is presented with a combined categorisation task (consisting of four categories: a task-specific category and a word category). The participant performs this task twice: once, when one task-specific category is paired with a positively connoted word (e.g., "health or pleasant words"), and the other with a negatively connoted word (e.g., "health or unpleasant words"). Then, reverse categorisation occurs: the first task-specific category is paired with a negatively connoted word, and the second with a positively connoted word. A shorter reaction time for a stimulus belonging to a conceptual category paired with a positive word and a longer reaction time when the same stimulus appears with a negative word indicates a more positive implicit attitude towards this category than the other category used in the study. In addition to reaction times, the computer also records task accuracy (see Chapter 1). The IAT also has a number of variants, but the basic idea of this method is retained in all of them. It should also be emphasised that correlations between attitude measures based on self-reports and the IAT are generally weakly correlated (see Hofmann et al., 2005).

10.5 Physiological Measures

Physiological measures address the physiological correlates of evaluative responses. Since people do not have (at least full) control over their physiological responses, their measurements are considered to overcome the shortcomings of self-report (Cunningham et al., 2008).

One of the first physiological measures used in relation to attitudes was the galvanic skin response. This measure records changes in the electrical conductivity of the skin, which are related to sympathetic nervous system activity and reflect the body's reactions to emotional or physical stimuli. However, research results (e.g., Cacioppo & Sandman, 1981) have shown that galvanic skin response primarily measures arousal, but it is difficult or even impossible to determine whether this arousal results from a positive or negative stimulus based on this measurement. This is unless the stimulus presented to individuals is unambiguous, for example, unambiguously aversive or anxiety-inducing.

A more promising physiological method for measuring posture is the analysis of subtle facial muscle activity, particularly around the mouth and eyebrows – facial electromyography (EMG; e.g., Cacioppo et al., 1986). The main premise of EMG is that when people are confronted with a given object, their reactions to it are emotional, which is reflected in facial expressions. These expressions are often so subtle that they are imperceptible. However, by attaching electrodes to specific areas of the face, patterns of facial muscle activation can be recorded, allowing the valence and intensity of people's emotional responses to be determined. In turn, based on people's emotional responses to these stimuli, it can be inferred whether attitudes are positive or negative. The problem with the widespread use of EMG is that it is a laboratory-based measurement, requiring technical knowledge and equipment.

10.6 Brain Activity Measurements

Technological advances have also provided more advanced brain imaging tools. These enable the analysis of which brain regions are engaged and how they are engaged during the initiation and progression of evaluative responses.

Techniques used to measure attitudes in relation to brain activity are procedures based on event-related brain potentials (ERPs; e.g., Cacioppo et al., 1996). ERPs refer to a specific pattern of electrical activity in the cerebral cortex (measured by electrodes attached to specific areas of the skull) during the categorisation of a sequence of objects. Large ERPs occur when a person has already categorised a sequence of objects according to a certain context (e.g., positive) and encounters an object inconsistent with this categorisation (stimulus, e.g., negative). These are called late positive potentials (LLPs). Small ERPs, however, occur when the object's categorisation is consistent with previously classified items. The amplitude of the LLP wave therefore changes as a function of the difference between the valence of the stimuli and the valence of the context. ERPs are relatively frequently used, especially to determine the coherence and affective valence of attitude responses. Furthermore, the LPP measure enables precise analysis of evaluative processing time and is resistant to deliberative evaluation bias.

Studies using functional magnetic resonance imaging (fMRI) complement ERP measurements by providing insights into which brain regions activity occurs related to the task being performed or the perceived stimulus (e.g., Cunningham et al., 2004).

In summary, perhaps the most striking aspect of attitude measurement is the wide variety of procedures available to those who wish to measure them. Each of the methods described has advantages and disadvantages. Furthermore, some methods may be useful in one context but completely useless in others. Nevertheless, these methods constitute a rather capacious “toolbox” from which we can choose what seems most useful for our purposes – both theoretical and practical.

Further Readings

Krosnick, J. A., Judd, C. M., & Wittenbrink, B. (2019). The measurement of attitudes. In D. Albarracín, & B. T. Johnson (Eds.), *Handbook of attitudes, Volume 1: Basic principles* (pp. 45–105). New York: Routledge.

References

Cacioppo, J. T., & Sandman, C. A. (1981). Psychophysiological functioning, cognitive responding, and attitudes. In R. E. Petty, T. M. Ostrom, & T. C. Brock (Eds.), *Cognitive responses in persuasion* (pp. 81–103). Hillsdale, NJ: Lawrence Erlbaum.

Cacioppo, J. T., Crites, S. L., & Gardner, W. L. (1996). Attitudes to the right: Evaluative processing is associated with lateralized late positive event-related brain potentials. *Personality and Social Psychology Bulletin, 22*(12), 1205–1219.

Cacioppo, J. T., Petty, R. E., Losch, M. E., & Kim, H. S. (1986). Electromyographic activity over facial muscle regions can differentiate the valence and intensity of affective reactions. *Journal of Personality and Social Psychology, 50*(2), 260–268.

Crites, S. L., Fabrigar, L. R., & Petty, R. E. (1994). Measuring the affective and cognitive properties of attitudes: Conceptual and methodological issues. *Personality and Social Psychology Bulletin, 20*(6), 619–634.

Cunningham, W. A., Packer, D. J., Kesek, A., & Van Bavel, J. J. (2008). Implicit measurement of attitudes: A physiological approach. In R. E. Petty, R. H. Fazio, & P. Briñol (Eds.), *Attitudes: Insights from the new implicit measures* (pp. 485–512). New York: Psychology Press.

Cunningham, W. A., Raye, C. L., & Johnson, M. K. (2004). Implicit and explicit evaluation: fMRI correlates of valence, emotional intensity, and control in the processing of attitudes. *Journal of Cognitive Neuroscience, 16*(10), 1717–1729.

Cwalina, W., Falkowski, A., & Newman, B. I. (2015). *Political marketing: Theoretical and strategic foundations.* New York: Routledge.

Fazio, R. H., Sanbonmatsu, D. M., Powell, M. C., & Kardes, F. R. (1986). On the automatic activation of attitudes. *Journal of Personality and Social Psychology, 50*(2), 229–238.

Greenwald, A. G., McGhee, D. E., & Schwartz, J. L. K. (1998). Measuring individual differences in implicit cognition: The implicit association test. *Journal of Personality and Social Psychology, 74*(6), 1464–1480.

Hofmann, W., Gawronski, B., Gschwendner, T., Le, H., & Schmitt, M. (2005). A meta-analysis of the correlation between the Implicit Association Test and explicit self-report measures. *Personality and Social Psychology Bulletin, 31*(1), 1369–1385.

Koniak, P., & Cwalina, W. (2022). Forbid/allow asymmetry in persuasion: The forbid frame decreases biased elaboration and increases attitude change. *Social Psychology, 53*(1), 1–20.

Krosnick, J. A. (1999). Survey research. *Annual Review of Psychology, 50*, 537–567.

Krosnick, J. A., Judd, C. M., & Wittenbrink, B. (2019). The measurement of attitudes. In D. Albarracín, & B. T. Johnson (Eds.), *Handbook of attitudes, Volume 1: Basic principles* (pp. 45–105). New York: Routledge.

Likert, R. (1932). A technique for the measurement of attitudes. *Archives of Psychology, 140,* 1–55.

Nisbett, R. E., & Wilson, T. D. (1977). Telling more than we can know: Verbal reports on mental processes. *Psychological Review, 84*(3), 231–259.

Osgood, C. E., Suci, G. J., & Tannenbaum, P. H. (1957). *The measurement of meaning.* Urbana, IL: University of Illinois Press.

Pennebaker, J. W., Booth, R. J., & Francis, M. E. (2007). *LIWC2007: Linguistic inquiry and word count.* Austin, TX: LIWC.net.

Rocklage, M. D., & Fazio, R. H. (2015). The evaluative lexicon: Adjective use as a means of assessing and distinguishing attitude valence, extremity, and emotionality. *Journal of Experimental Social Psychology, 56,* 214–227.

Rugg, D. (1941). Experiments in wording questions: II. *Public Opinion Quarterly, 5*(1), 91–92.

Schuman, H., & Presser, S. (1981). *Questions and answers in attitude surveys: Experiments on question form, wording and context.* Thousand Oaks, CA: Sage Publications.

Thurstone, L. L. (1928). Attitudes can be measured. *American Journal of Sociology, 33,* 529–554.

Part 4

Key Impacts on Research and Practice

This section in summary

- The specifics of persuasion in advertising, including the role of message repetition and the facts and myths surrounding subliminal persuasion
- The health-related consequences of attitudes and the effectiveness of gain- versus loss-framed messages, fear appeals, and metaphors in persuasion
- The interplay between attitudes towards politicians/parties and towards issues and political proposals, as well as the role of priming, framing and emotion in political persuasion
- The role of prejudice and affective polarisation in intergroup relations, ways of changing negative intergroup attitudes, and the usefulness of the paradoxical thinking strategy
- The specifics of environmental attitudes and their links to pro-environmental behaviours

DOI: 10.4324/9781003589174-14

Chapter 11

Attitudes and Persuasion in Society

11.1 Advertising

Advertising can be defined as "any form of paid communication by an identified sponsor aimed to inform and/or persuade target audiences about an organization, product, service or idea" (Fennis & Stroebe, 2010, p. 2). It can be seen as a specific form of persuasion, and in fact many principles of persuasion have been tested with use of advertising communication. As the above definition states, one of the core functions of advertising is to inform. The first step in persuading people, particularly when the product is new or when they are unaware of the issue (as in health or environmental campaigns), is to **raise awareness** of it. Once this has been achieved, advertisements must foster positive (or negative, if the goal is to discourage people from doing something) attitudes towards the product or issue, and ensure that these attitudes are strong. If people have a positive attitude towards a brand, they are more likely to choose it over competitors' brands, provided this attitude is easily accessible. However, if the attitude is positive but weak, the probability of choosing this brand is low (Priester et al., 2004). Furthermore, once a product or brand has established its position, the role of advertising is to **maintain top-of-mind awareness and encourage loyalty** (see Fennis & Stroebe, 2010, for a wider discussion of the effects of advertising).

Advertising, particularly that relating to consumer goods, products, and brands, operates within a specific context. The people it is aimed at are often only weakly interested in processing it. In fact, they may even try to avoid it. There are various reasons for this. Advertising can be perceived as intrusive and hinder the receiver's goals. For example, it can

> **Top-of-mind awareness.** A type of brand or product awareness whereby a specific brand or product comes to mind as one of the first when a consumer is asked about a specific industry, product, or service category.

DOI: 10.4324/9781003589174-15

disrupt film viewing on TV or appear on a webpage when someone is trying to read the news. Furthermore, the sheer quantity of advertising may be seen as excessive – a phenomenon known as **perceived ad clutter** – which is common in competitive advertising environments (Cho & Cheon, 2004). This can result in advertising receiving **little attention**, and even prompting **ad avoidance behaviours**. One strategy to overcome this is to use **attention-grabbing tactics**, such as distinctive colours or sizes. However, such attempts to grab attention may backfire if they are perceived as too intrusive, leading to the inference of manipulative intent and decreased persuasiveness (Campbell, 1995). Moreover, some evidence suggests that advertising can be effective even when the recipient is not paying much attention (Santoso et al., 2020). According to dual-process theories of persuasion (see Chapter 7), various peripheral or heuristic cues should be employed in such circumstances, such as celebrity endorsements or pleasant music evoking positive associations. Some researchers even suggest that advertising primarily influences brand attitudes through its emotional content. Moreover, although emotional content is easily processed at lower levels of attention, increasing attention weakens its effect (Heath et al., 2006).

Perceived ad clutter. Consumers' subjective feeling that the quantity of advertising is excessive.

Resistance-promoting heuristics. Mental shortcuts that people use to resist persuasion. Activated by various situational cues, they allow people to quickly reject persuasive messages without elaborating them.

Importantly, advertising is often clearly distinguished from the surrounding content, sometimes even being labelled as persuasive content. This may prompt the recipient to resist (see Chapter 8). This context of influence activates **resistance-promoting heuristics**. To resist persuasion successfully, self-control is usually required. However, when the resistance-promoting heuristic is activated, people with low self-control are more likely to resist persuasion than those with high self-control. This is because those with low self-control tend to mindlessly rely on the heuristics that facilitate compliance or promote resistance, depending on which has been activated (Janssen & Fennis, 2017).

11.1.1 Repetition in Persuasion and Advertising

One of the defining features of advertising is the repetition of messages, which can occur within a relatively short period of time. For instance, a viewer may see the same advertisement several times while watching

Illusion of truth (also illusory truth effect). Tendency to perceive repeated statements as more valid than new ones, regardless of whether they are true.

Spacing of messages. The time interval between each exposure to a repeated message (e.g., an advertisement).

a film on TV, or notice the same advertisement on different billboards during their commute. Depending on what is being measured, this repetition can have various effects. The increased **feeling of familiarity** can create the **illusion of truth**, whereby repeated statements are perceived as more valid than new ones, regardless of their truthfulness (Moons et al., 2009). It may also improve **recall** of advertising content (Schmidt & Eisend, 2015). As studies on mere exposure (see Section 3.2) have shown, frequent exposure to an object can lead to a higher evaluation of it. However, when it comes to attitudes, more does not necessarily mean better. Overall, the relationship between repeated advertising and attitude towards the product takes the form of an inverted U: while initial exposure improves attitude, further exposure beyond this point decreases persuasiveness. The **spacing of messages** – that is, the time between each exposure to advertising – is an important factor affecting the effectiveness of repeated advertising. Repetition has a stronger effect on attitudes when exposures to advertising are spaced rather than massed (i.e., repeated continuously without a break between repetitions) (Schmidt & Eisend, 2015).

From the perspective of the elaboration likelihood model (see Section 7.1), repetition provides a better opportunity to scrutinise the merits of the advocated position or object. When the argumentation presented is strong, repetition increases the persuasiveness of the message. For weak argumentation, however, it decreases persuasiveness. However, repeating strong arguments becomes less effective once a certain exposure threshold has been reached. Increasing repetition from three to five times stimulates counterargumentation (Cacioppo & Petty, 1985). Therefore, moderate repetition increases analytical processing, resulting in greater persuasion when strong arguments are used rather than weak ones. However, the personal relevance of the message to the audience can moderate this effect. Repetition can increase analytical processing when relevance is high. However, it can reduce analytical processing when relevance is low (Claypool et al., 2004). Furthermore, when processing is low, repetition can make both strong and weak arguments appear more persuasive. This is because familiarity increases with repetition (Moons et al., 2009).

11.1.2 Subliminal Advertising

In one episode of the crime series *Columbo* (season 3, episode 4, titled "Double Exposure"), an advertising expert uses subliminal cuts to blackmail people and help him commit murder. This reflects the fears raised by research into subliminal advertising that was allegedly conducted prior to the episode being broadcast. The researcher claimed to have boosted popcorn and Coca-Cola sales by displaying the words "eat popcorn" and "drink Coca-Cola" on cinema screens for 1/3,000 of a second during film screenings. However, this study was never actually conducted, and the results were fabricated. Furthermore, nobody has been able to replicate the claimed results. Nevertheless, the study raised public concerns about unwittingly becoming a victim of manipulation (Broyles, 2006).

As Broyles (2006) points out, for something to qualify as subliminal advertising, the stimulus (e.g., a brand name) must be below an individual's level of conscious awareness. In research practice, the technique of subliminal priming is employed. This "involves presenting people with single words or images at a speed that is below the conscious threshold" (Smarandescu & Shimp, 2015, p. 717). Such words (e.g., brand names) may be presented for a very short time (e.g., 23 ms), preceded and followed by a string of masking letters (e.g., XXXXXXX), which are presented for a longer time (e.g., 500 ms). Participants are led to believe that their task is to detect specific letters hidden within a string of other letters (e.g., lowercase b's within a string of capital B's). To make matters even more obscure, participants are informed that the string of Xs serves as an orienting cue prior to each string of Bs. As this example shows, it is a rather artificial situation, far removed from inserting one frame into a cinema film.

However, research using this method has found that subliminal persuasion can be effective in certain specific cases. Strahan with collaborators (2002) demonstrated that, when individuals are motivated to achieve a particular goal (e.g., when they are thirsty), such priming can be effective by activating cognitions related to the goal and increasing its priority. For example, priming thirst with words such as "thirst" and "dry" caused participants to drink more liquid if they were thirsty (after eating cookies without drinking water), but not when they were not thirsty (when they could wash the cookies down with as much water as they wanted). Furthermore, priming thirst increased participants' evaluation of a sports drink that was advertised as effective in quenching thirst but had no effect on their evaluation of a sports drink advertised as effective in restoring electrolytes. Without priming, participants evaluated both drinks similarly. Other studies have found that priming a drink brand (e.g., Lipton Ice) increases the intention to drink the primed brand and the likelihood of choosing it but only for thirsty participants (Karremans et al., 2006).

Further Reading

Fennis, B. M., & Stroebe, W. (2010). *The psychology of advertising*. London: Psychology Press.

11.2 Health

Attitudes play a role in shaping behaviours and decisions that affect our health. According to Sweeny and Rankin (2018), the prevailing theoretical basis for many studies on attitudes in health contexts is the **theory of planned behaviour** (TPB; see Section 4.3.1). This theory describes three categories of determinants of intentions to engage in a given behaviour: subjective norms, perceived behavioural control, and attitude towards the behaviour. Various health-related areas in which attitudes play a role have been studied, including cancer, HIV/AIDS, substance use (e.g., tobacco, alcohol, or drugs), diet, and physical activity (Albarracín & Johnson, 2018).

Attitudes influence behaviours relating to the prevention and screening of diseases and injuries, as well as treatment decisions (Sweeny & Rankin, 2018). **Primary prevention** involves avoiding exposure to hazards (e.g., wearing sun protection or protective masks), altering unhealthy or unsafe behaviours (e.g., quitting smoking or increasing vegetable intake), and boosting immunity (e.g., through vaccination). For instance, positive attitudes towards tanning are linked to spending more time in the sun and using less sun protection. Conversely, positive attitudes towards sun protection are related to more frequent sunscreen use (Sweeny & Rankin, 2018). Interest in **attitudes towards vaccination** (as well as other protective behaviours, such as social distancing and wearing masks) increased during the COVID-19 pandemic. However, many studies also focused on attitudes towards HPV and influenza vaccinations, as well as general attitudes towards vaccinating children (Yaqub et al., 2014). One area of interest was attitudes towards **mandatory vaccination** and how to prevent possible reactance towards such requirements. While some studies have found that mandatory vaccination increases the intention to vaccinate (Albarracín et al., 2021), others have found that mandatory vaccination policies accompanied by sanctions for non-compliance evoke reactance (Kriss et al., 2022). These conflicting results may be explained by how the regulation is formulated, that is, whether it is perceived as absolute (see Section 8.1.4). Other studies have shown that compulsory vaccination increases reactance among people with negative attitudes towards vaccination but has no effect on the attitudes of

> **Primary prevention**. Avoiding exposure to hazards, altering unhealthy or unsafe behaviours, and boosting immunity.

those with positive views (Betsch & Böhm, 2016). Schmid with collaborators (2024) presented various interventions that may be less threatening to individual autonomy than vaccination mandates (e.g., persuasion).

Screening behaviours (secondary prevention). Actions whose goal is to detect diseases at the earliest possible stage.

Bellicose metaphors. Speaking about disease in war-related terms, referring to it as an enemy and treatment as a battle, etc.

The aim of **screening behaviours** (secondary prevention) is to detect diseases at the earliest possible stage. Attitudes towards such testing may be negative due to the perception that certain procedures are unpleasant or uncomfortable. One source of negative attitudes towards cancer screening is cancer fatalism, that is, the belief that a cancer diagnosis is tantamount to a death sentence (Cohen, 2022). Attitudes are also related to preferences for various treatments and adherence to health maintenance plans.

11.2.1 Health Persuasion

Although health-related persuasion is also used in **doctor-patient communication**, research mostly focuses on **large-scale campaigns**. The findings of Hauser and Schwarz (2015, 2020) highlight the importance of basing decisions relating to health communication and persuasion on research. They demonstrated that **bellicose metaphors**, which are widely used in public discourse around cancer (e.g., "the war on cancer", "fighting cancer", "cancer as an enemy"), can have serious side effects in the absence of positive ones. These metaphors do not increase intentions to monitor (e.g., undergo testing), bolster oneself (e.g., eat fruit and vegetables), or seek treatment (e.g., accept various treatment options in case of eventual diagnosis). Furthermore, they reduce the intention to engage in self-limiting preventive behaviours (e.g., eating fewer fatty foods). They also lead to cancer treatment being perceived as more challenging and increase fatalistic beliefs about cancer prevention ("If someone is meant to get cancer, they will get it no matter what they do").

11.2.1.1 Gain Framing versus Loss Framing

Health-promoting messages can focus on the positive aspects of certain behaviours (**gain framing**), or on the negative consequences of inaction (**loss framing**). For example, a gain-framed message might indicate that

Gain framing. Describing the positive aspects of certain behaviours.

Loss framing. Describing the negative consequences of inaction.

a blood test can reveal one's current cholesterol level, or that vaccination can reduce the risk of contracting genital HPV. Similarly, a loss-framed message might highlight the potential consequences of not taking a blood test, such as missing the opportunity to find out one's cholesterol level, or of not getting vaccinated, which could increase the risk of contracting HPV. Rothman and Salovey (1997, 2007) proposed **tailoring the framing of messages to the type of health behaviour** being advocated (see also Section 12.1). They concluded that loss-framed messages are more effective when advocating detection behaviours. Conversely, gain-framed messages are more effective in persuading people to engage in promotional behaviours (primary prevention).

However, it seems that loss- and gain-framed appeals are generally equally persuasive, although the specifics of the behaviour in question may play a role. Gain-framed messages have been found to be more effective than loss-framed messages in promoting dental hygiene behaviours, but not behaviours relating to safe sex, skin cancer prevention or diet and nutrition (O'Keefe & Jensen, 2007). When it comes to encouraging vaccination, gain- and loss-framed appeals are persuasive to a similar extent overall. However, some results suggest that loss-framed messages may be more effective than gain-framed ones in persuading parents to vaccinate their children (O'Keefe & Nan, 2012). Loss-framed messages have been shown to be more effective in encouraging breast cancer detection behaviours, but not other types of detection behaviours, such as skin cancer or dental problem detection (O'Keefe & Jensen, 2009).

Furthermore, loss-framed messages may worsen the negative relationship between **conspiracy beliefs** and attitudes towards recommended preventive behaviours, such as wearing masks, as well as detection behaviours, such as testing. Thus, they may encourage those who believe in conspiracy theories to reject such recommendations. When conspiracy beliefs are prevalent, as during the COVID-19 pandemic, the gain frame may be more effective than the loss frame. However, some evidence suggests that the loss frame may be a more effective way of promoting detection behaviours for people who do not endorse a conspiracy worldview (Cwalina & Koniak, 2023).

Furthermore, Maheswaran and Meyers-Levy (1990) proposed that the effectiveness of framing depends on the **level of involvement** in the issue. When issue involvement is low (e.g., when people believe they are not in the at-risk group), people rely on simple cues; one such cue may be the framing of the message. Since people generally accept positive information and reject negative information, a gain-framed message is more persuasive than a loss-framed message in situations of low involvement. However, when issue involvement is high (e.g., when people believe they are in the at-risk group), the message is processed more systematically. Since negative information is generally more persuasive than positive information, loss-framed messages are more effective for highly involved individuals. Moreover, highly involved receivers only find loss-framed messages more persuasive than gain-framed ones when the advocated prevention has some **risky implications** (i.e., an undesirable effect rather than a desirable one). When the risky implication is low, highly involved people are equally persuaded by gain- and loss-framed messages (Meyers-Levy & Maheswaran, 2004).

11.2.1.2 Fear Appeals

Health-related persuasion often involves indicating that the recipient's health is under threat. The aim is to evoke fear in order to motivate the recipient to change their behaviour or take protective action. Various models have described how fear appeals work. We will briefly describe two of these models (for more detailed reviews of these and others, see Mongeau, 2012; Shen & Dillard, 2014; Witte & Allen, 2000).

According to **Protection Motivation Theory** (e.g., Maddux & Rogers, 1983), fear appeals prompt cognitive **appraisal processes** concerning the **severity** of the threat and the individual's **susceptibility** to it (i.e., the probability of it happening to them). They also prompt an **appraisal of the effectiveness** of the recommended coping strategy, as well as an assessment of the individual's **self-efficacy** in implementing it (i.e., whether they perceive themselves as capable of changing their diet). These processes arouse protection motivation, which in turn shapes the persuasive effectiveness of the fear appeal. Overall, fear appeals are most effective when the perceived threat (in terms of severity and susceptibility) and the perceived efficacy of the response (in terms of both response efficacy and self-efficacy) are both high.

The **extended parallel process model** (e.g., Witte, 1992; Witte & Allen, 2000) suggests that the initial response to a message intended to provoke fear involves **evaluating the threat**. If the receiver perceives the threat as irrelevant or low, they are not motivated to process the message and may simply ignore it. However, when the threat is perceived as high and relevant, fear is evoked and the receiver seeks actions that will **reduce this fear**. If they perceive the efficacy of the proposed response as high (i.e., if they believe it is effective and have high self-efficacy), they will try to control the threat by thinking of ways to remove or lessen it. In most cases, they adopt the course of action proposed by the message. However, if the recipient believes that they are **unable to cope** with the threat or that the recommended action will not work, they will look for other ways to control their fear. They may react with denial of the threat ("it won't happen to me"), defensive avoidance ("I'm not going to think about it"), or reactance ("it's just pharmaceutical industry nonsense").

Efficacy statements. Statements included in fear appeals that assure recipients of their ability to perform the recommended actions.

Overall, fear appeals are effective. A meta-analysis conducted by Tannenbaum and collaborators (2015) indicates that their effectiveness can be increased when the message includes **efficacy statements**. In other words, the message should assure the audience that they are capable of performing the recommended actions (self-efficacy) and/or that these actions will have positive outcomes (response efficacy). Furthermore, such messages are more effective when they depict high susceptibility (i.e., emphasise the receiver's personal risk) and/or severity (i.e., describe the negative consequences of not taking action; for example, cigarette packets could feature vivid images of infected body parts). However, some research suggests that **severity information** is the least important component of fear appeals. In fact, it may even have the opposite effect, leading to defensive responses (Ruiter et al., 2014).

Fear-based messages are more effective when the recommended behaviour is a one-off, such as vaccination, than when the behaviour is repeated, such as regular exercise. Nevertheless, they are still effective enough to influence repeated behaviours. Furthermore, fear appeals appear to be more effective when the target audience is predominantly female. Some research also suggests that arousing too little or too much fear can reduce the persuasiveness of the message (the **curvilinear hypothesis**; see Shen & Dillard, 2014). Other studies indicate that there is a threshold above which depicting additional fear does not lead to more persuasive results, though it is not detrimental (Tannenbaum et al., 2015). Nevertheless, a moderate level of fear seems optimal for persuasion.

Further Readings

Atkin, C., & Salmon, C. T. (2012). Persuasive strategies in health campaigns. In J. P. Dillard, & L. Shen (Eds.), *Persuasive strategies in health campaigns* (2nd ed., pp. 278–295). Thousand Oaks, CA: Sage Publications.

Leventhal, H., Cameron, L., Leventhal, E. A., & Ozakinci, G. (2005). Do messages from your body, your friends, your doctor, or the media shape your health behavior? In T. C. Brock & M. C. Green (Eds.), *Persuasion: Psychological insights and perspectives* (2nd ed., pp. 195–223). Thousand Oaks, CA: Sage Publications.

11.3 Politics

In politics persuasion is used to change attitudes towards two main classes of objects. The first of these are **attitudes towards issues, policy proposals, or regulations**. Examples of these issues include euthanasia, EU membership, immigration, raising the retirement age, and the construction of nuclear power plants. The second class comprises **political actors, such as politicians and political parties**, who are also objects of attitudes that can be modified through persuasion. The processes of forming and changing attitudes towards issues, politicians, and parties are often interrelated. Moreover, in candidate- and image-based politics, it seems that attitudes towards politicians or parties have become the primary object of persuasion. Attitudes towards issues, proposals, or regulations appear to play a secondary, or even instrumental, role as these topics are often discussed to foster favourable attitudes towards the politician or party in question (Cwalina & Koniak, 2025a). Nevertheless, discussion around issues such as immigration, education, or neighbourly relations affects public attitudes towards them, even when they are treated instrumentally.

When a politician tries to persuade voters about an issue or policy proposal, the voters' attitudes towards that politician may also change. Attitudes towards the source can change as a result of the language used; for example, **powerful versus powerless language**. Powerless speech is characterised by hedges, hesitations, polite forms, disclaimers, and tag questions, whereas powerful speech lacks such features. Overall, powerless speech reduces the effectiveness of persuasion, although it can sometimes be beneficial (Blankenship & Holtgraves, 2005). Speakers may deliberately use some of these powerless forms to increase elaboration (see Blankenship & Craig, 2011) or to avoid the recipient's reactance (see Section 8.1). However, such a speech style may also negatively affect attitudes towards the speaker, decreasing their perceived competence and attractiveness (Hosman & Siltanen, 2006). Similarly, using **two-sided messages** (see Section 5.3.2) can result in a more effective change in attitude towards the subject of the message, as well as increasing the credibility of the source (Bohner et al., 2003). The attitude towards the speaker may also be affected by the topic chosen for the message or its valence (where the positivity or negativity can transfer to the evaluation of the speaker).

However, attitudes towards parties or politicians are significant factors in shaping attitudes towards policy proposals. In politics, the **partisanship** of the source is particularly important. People can develop a positive view of policy proposals simply because their party has endorsed them. Furthermore, even when a policy proposal aligns with the recipient's ideological stance and is evaluated positively in the absence of information about the supporting party, it can be rejected solely because it is proposed by the opposing party or opposed by their own. Conversely, people may accept a policy they would otherwise reject if their party supports it. Overall, when partisanship cues are present, people do not base their attitudes on the objective content of policies. Furthermore, while people readily acknowledge that others, particularly those who support the opposing party, are influenced by partisan information, they deny that information about party support affects their evaluation of policy proposals (Cohen, 2003).

11.3.1 Priming

People cannot base their evaluations and judgements on all the relevant evidence available to them. Instead, they rely on the information that is accessible to them when thinking about the evaluated object. **Priming** works by increasing the **accessibility** of certain knowledge structures and consequently increasing their influence on attitudes. Priming is generally defined as the phenomenon whereby exposure to one object (person, picture, information, etc.) influences the interpretation, evaluation, or choice of a subsequent object (Cwalina et al., 2015; Iyengar & Kinder, 1987). For instance, after watching news reports about rising crime rates, people may judge political parties or politicians based on their perceived ability to combat crime. However, after seeing news about the worsening state of the economy, their economic competencies may become a more crucial factor. Therefore, the basic effect of priming is not a change in how the object's attributes are perceived and evaluated, but rather an increase in the influence of some of these attributes on the attitude towards the object. While priming does not change people's perceptions of politicians' competencies or image, it does change the evaluation criteria and which of these competencies or traits will influence the overall attitude more.

Changes in the criteria and standards on which people base their attitudes towards candidates, parties, issues, or policy proposals may result from exposure to media content. The media tends to cover some issues more than others. As a result, issues that receive more coverage are considered more important by viewers (the **agenda-setting effect**). However, this also makes the **issue** more accessible in an individual's memory. Consequently, the media affect the criteria used to evaluate political entities, thereby shaping these evaluations. Politicians also intentionally engage

> **Priming.** Phenomenon whereby exposure to one object influences the interpretation, evaluation, or choice of a subsequent object.
>
> **Agenda-setting effect.** An increase in the perceived importance of issues that the media focuses on.

in priming by giving certain issues more prominence in their statements. This is an attempt to increase the weight voters put on these issues when choosing between candidates or parties (Druckman et al., 2004). Politicians or parties tend to prime issues that are relatively novel but easy for the public to understand and that are important to them. Furthermore, issues on which candidates and parties have clear and distinct positions that are supported by the public are primed more effectively.

Priming may also relate to a candidate's **personal attributes**, such as trustworthiness or integrity (Druckman et al., 2004). This can be achieved by emphasising the importance of certain traits when evaluating candidates (e.g., indicating that the candidate should be trustworthy, particularly if their opponent is perceived as being less so). It can also be done indirectly, for example, by displaying the national flag to emphasise patriotism, or by highlighting issues related to the candidate's image. For instance, discussing childcare could emphasise protectiveness as a criterion of evaluation.

Priming may also affect **attitudes towards issues** (for other examples of priming see Cwalina & Koniak, 2025b). For instance, exposure to negative stereotypes of certain groups (through photographs or rap music, i.e.) may reduce support for social assistance programmes aimed at those groups (Johnson et al., 2009).

11.3.2 Framing

Most issues discussed in society can be viewed from various perspectives. For example, budget cuts could be considered in terms of their economic consequences, such as reducing public debt, or their social consequences, such as reducing funding for public schools. **Framing** is "the process by which a communication source constructs and defines social or political issue for its audience" (Nelson et al., 1997, p. 221). This can be achieved by making changes to certain parts of a message, such as headings, conclusions, or even individual words, while keeping the factual information unchanged. Consequently, framing influences "the process by which people develop a particular conceptualization of an issue or reorient their thinking about an issue" (Chong & Druckman, 2007, p. 104), and can **change attitudes** towards a given issue (see also Section 11.2.1).

For example, Simon and Jerit (2007) presented their participants an article describing partial-birth abortion. In one version, the word "foetus" was used 16 times, while in the

Framing. The process by which a source of communication constructs and defines an issue for its receivers.

other version, it had been replaced with "baby." Apart from this substitution, the articles were identical. Participants who read the version containing the word "foetus" expressed less support for a ban on partial-birth abortion than those who read the version with the word "baby" (whose attitudes, in turn, were similar to those of the control group, who did not read the article). In Druckman's (2001) experiment, participants read an article about the Ku Klux Klan's request to hold a rally on a university campus. The body of the articles was identical, except for the titles, headlines, pictures, and quoted opinions at the end of the text. These differences framed the issue as either a matter of free speech (e.g., "Klan Tests University's Commitment to Free Speech") or as a matter of public safety (e.g., "Possible Klan Rally Raises Safety Concerns"). Attitudes towards allowing the rally were more positive among participants who read the article framed in terms of free speech than among those who read the version framed in terms of public safety. However, the framing of the article only influenced readers' opinions when it came from a credible source (*The New York Times*). When the source was non-credible (*The National Enquirer*) framing has no consequence for receivers reactions, which may suggest that framing works "because citizens delegate to credible elites for guidance" (p. 1061).

Framing also affects receivers' **cognitive reactions** (see Section 7.1). First, it reduces the number of reactions, showing that frames reduce the extent to which receivers think about the issue. Second, it focuses receivers' thoughts on the value invoked by the frame (e.g., equality), resulting in this value being invoked more frequently in their responses. Thus, framing both focuses and narrows citizens' thoughts (Brewer & Gross, 2005). Furthermore, other studies have shown that framing works by increasing the perceived importance of the values invoked by the frame (e.g., Druckman, 2001).

11.3.3 Emotions

Political persuasion exploits emotions evoked by both external factors and persuasive messages. Three emotions that are frequently addressed in the context of political persuasion are fear (or anxiety), enthusiasm, and anger. **Fear and anxiety** lead to a positive bias when assessing policy proposals presented as protective measures against threats, such as those related to health or terrorism. As a result, support increases and rejection decreases, even for propositions that would otherwise be unacceptable (Koniak & Cwalina, 2020, 2025). Furthermore, anxiety increases attention towards political campaigns and enhances learning (Marcus & Mackuen, 1993). Brader (2005) demonstrated that negative political advertisements featuring **fear-evoking cues** (e.g., discordant music or black-and-white images of violence) were more effective in persuading people to vote for the advert's sponsor than similar negative advertisements without such cues. Moreover, evoked fear reduces reliance on previous preferences and increases the likelihood of basing the choice on evaluations of candidates' issues and traits. Thus, to some degree, fear cancels out the motivated bolstering of initial attitudes.

According to Marcus and Mackuen (1993), **enthusiasm** enhances involvement and interest in a campaign. Furthermore, compared to positive advertisements, ads with **enthusiasm-evoking cues** (e.g., uplifting music and colourful images of children) led to an increase in reliance on prior preferences and strengthened prior convictions. Therefore, while enthusiasm increases support for the advert's sponsor among existing supporters, it also increases opposition among existing opponents (Brader, 2005). In other words, it is counterproductive if the aim is to change someone's mind, but it can embolden existing supporters. To some extent, **anger** has a similar effect to enthusiasm in that it motivates a biased evaluation of information. It impairs information processing and openness to new information. Angered people favour information that is consistent with their pre-existing attitudes and disapprove of information that is inconsistent with them. Anger also amplifies the initial evaluation of policy proposals. In the case of positively evaluated proposals, anger is associated with increased support. However, with negatively evaluated proposals, anger is associated with decreased support or increased rejection (Koniak & Cwalina, 2025).

Further Reading

Cwalina, W., Falkowski, A., & Newman, B. I. (2015). Persuasion in the political context: Opportunities and threats. In D. W. Stewart (Ed.), *Handbook of persuasion and social marketing, Vol. 1: Historical and social foundations* (pp. 61–128). Santa Barbara, CA: Praeger.

11.4 Intergroup Relations

Although people are all unique, they also belong to many different groups. For instance, an individual could be an employee of Department A, male or female, a member of Family B, and Polish or French. They may also be a member of Church C, vote for Party D and support Football Team E. People may also form groups based on their beliefs and attitudes towards various issues. Examples include people who don't vaccinate their children, pro-lifers versus pro-choicers, and feminists. The importance of belonging to a particular group varies from person to person and can also change depending on the situation. When a person identifies with a group, other people can be categorised as either members of the ingroup or various outgroups. Some of these outgroups are liked, while others are not.

Prejudice. A negative bias towards a social category of people.

Intergroup attitudes. Feelings, opinions, expectations, and beliefs about traits that members of a given group possess.

Stereotypes. Associations and attributions of specific characteristics to a group.

Most research on group attitudes focuses on prejudice. **Prejudice** is typically defined as "a negative bias toward a social category of people" (Paluck & Green, 2009, p. 339), resulting in discriminatory behaviour and/or intentions. However, it is not always negative towards the target group. It can also involve positive feelings towards an outgroup. However, this positivity can lead to behaviour that may be perceived as discriminatory. For example, asking an Asian person to solve a maths problem. Therefore, prejudice can be defined as "an individual-level attitude (whether subjectively positive or negative) toward groups and their members that creates or maintains hierarchical status relations between groups" (Dovidio et al., 2018, p. 420). Other research uses the term **intergroup attitudes**, which "refers to feelings, opinions, expectations, and beliefs about traits that members of a given group possess" (Brauer, 2024, p. 281). **Stereotypes**, which are conceptually related to prejudices, are defined as "associations and attributions of specific characteristics to a group" (Dovidio et al., 2018, p. 419). Thus, stereotypes are beliefs about the characteristics and traits of members of a given group. Although they can be inaccurate (like in case of national-character stereotypes) or may exaggerate group differences (e.g., political stereotypes), in many cases they are in fact accurate (e.g., demographic stereotypes related to race/ethnicity or gender). Moreover, people do not apply their stereotypes indiscriminately to all members of a given group. Rather, when they possess diagnostic information about an individual, they rely more on this information than on the stereotype (Jussim et al., 2015).

11.4.1 Sources and Consequences of Intergroup Attitudes

Intergroup attitudes are related to certain individual characteristics, such as **ideology**. However, the extent to which this ideology influences these attitudes varies depending on the target group. For example, both liberals and conservatives exhibit prejudice towards targets that are ideologically different rather than similar (Crawford et al., 2015). Furthermore, according to **social identity theory** (Tajfel & Turner, 1979), people fulfil their need for a positive identity by affiliating with valued groups and favourably distinguishing the ingroup from the outgroup. This can lead to social comparisons and motivational biases that affect intergroup relations. Intergroup attitudes are also shaped by **personal contact experiences** and various **social influence agents**, and how relations between groups are perceived by their members (for more mechanism and more detailed description, see Dovidio et al., 2018). For example, attitudes towards immigrants may result, among other factors, from whether politicians and media talk about immigrants and how they portray this group (usually as illegitimate, as bogus, as trying to cheat the system, and as potential terrorists or at least criminals) and from whether people perceive immigrants as threatening ("crime rate will rise") or competing ("they will take our jobs"; Esses, 2021).

Affective polarisation. The tendency to view supporters of opposing political parties negatively and supporters of one's own party positively.

Overall, people tend to perceive and evaluate outgroups more negatively than ingroups. Even when their attitudes towards a particular outgroup are neutral, people still show a preference for ingroup members. This tendency is evident in politics, for example. **Affective polarisation** is the tendency to view supporters of opposing political parties negatively and supporters of one's own party positively. This party-based affective polarisation is just as strong as race-based polarisation in American society. Moreover, it is driven more by outgroup animosity than ingroup favouritism (Iyengar & Westwood, 2015). Furthermore, while affective polarisation based on race or religion appears to be declining, partisan animosity is growing (Iyengar et al., 2012).

11.4.2 Reducing Negative Intergroup Attitudes

Although intergroup attitudes are difficult to change (Brauer, 2024), researchers and practitioners have tested many different ways of reducing prejudice (here we address only some examples that can be applied to persuasive interventions; for more extensive discussion, see Dovidio et al., 2018; Paluck & Green, 2009; Paluck et al., 2021). **Value consistency and self-worth interventions** involve reminding people of moral exemplars, provoking introspection about their beliefs and prejudices, or providing feedback on their level of prejudice. The idea is to evoke or increase people's desire to maintain a consistent and positive self-image (assuming they view prejudice as immoral) and encourage them to recognise that prejudice conflicts with some of their core values or traits (Paluck et al., 2021).

Conceptually similar interventions include **priming values or identities**. For instance, priming apolitical norms (e.g., priming military service members with the norms of political neutrality and the duty to defend all citizens, regardless of their political views) may reduce affective polarisation (Mullinix & Lythgoe, 2023). Similarly, affective polarisation and partisan hostility can be mitigated by priming national identity (Levendusky, 2018). However, priming national identity can backfire, strengthening negative attitudes towards immigrants (Wojcieszak & Garrett, 2018). Priming religious people with inclusive religious values (like "love the stranger as yourself" vs. exclusive ones, like "it is important to keep company with other people of my faith") lowers the perception of threat from a disliked group, leading to increased tolerance (Djupe & Calfano, 2013).

Other interventions attempt to **alter perceptions of category structures and the homogeneity of outgroups**. This can be achieved by presenting examples that challenge stereotypes about the outgroup, or by emphasising the diversity of opinions and characteristics within the group (Paluck et al., 2021). Brauer and his collaborators (2012) suggested that describing outgroup members in a heterogeneous manner is a more effective way of reducing prejudice than describing them positively. A message that says "some are hardworking and some are not" is less likely to provoke reactance than a message that argues "they are all hardworking." They also demonstrated that a simple poster seen by their participants while waiting for the experiment to begin was sufficiently persuasive. Participants who saw a poster containing both positive and negative characteristics of the outgroup (Arabs in France or African Americans in Canada) exhibited less prejudice towards this group than those exposed to a poster containing only positive traits. A comparison with the control group showed that the latter poster was ineffective.

11.4.3 Paradoxical Thinking and Changing Attitudes in the Context of Intractable Conflict

Conflict is a specific type of intergroup animosity. To implement any peaceful solutions, the beliefs and attitudes of both leaders and members of opposing groups must first be changed. The problem is that people become very entrenched in their beliefs and attitudes, especially when conflict is intractable. These attitudes and beliefs are often extreme and perpetuate the conflict. They are also organised into collective narratives, memories, and ethos. These narratives serve other functions too, such as maintaining a positive self-view, providing an understanding of the situation and justifying actions. Consequently, members of groups embroiled in an intractable conflict perceived as existential tend to be resistant to counterattitudinal information (Bar-Tal et al., 2021).

Paradoxical thinking strategy. Conveying a non-judgemental message that avoids direct evaluation or implication and is consistent with the recipient's attitudes and beliefs but which contains exaggerated or even absurd content.

Bar-Tal and his collaborators (2021) proposed that the **paradoxical thinking strategy** could be employed in such situations. This strategy involves conveying a message that is consistent with the recipient's attitudes and beliefs but which contains "amplified, exaggerated, or even absurd content" (p. 142). The message must also be non-judgemental, avoiding direct evaluations or implications. The aim is to elicit a surprising response from the recipient and prevent them from rejecting the message. Recognising the absurdity of the beliefs and attitudes expressed in the message should encourage the recipient to reconsider their own beliefs and attitudes. This, in turn, should lead to a sense of wrongness ("Can I really believe such an absurdity?") and may make the recipient open to change.

This strategy has been shown to be effective. For example, Hameiri and his colleagues (2014) tested it in the context of the Israeli-Palestinian conflict. Jewish Israelis who watched videos promoting paradoxical thinking (conveying messages such as "we need the conflict in order to have the strongest army in the world" and "in order to feel moral, we need the conflict") were more willing to re-evaluate their beliefs and reduce their perception of Palestinians' responsibility for the continuation of the conflict. Furthermore, subsequent studies have shown that this strategy is particularly effective for individuals with more extreme views and strong convictions (see Bar-Tal et al., 2021, for a review of other studies and a detailed description of the mechanism).

Further Reading

Dovidio, J. F., Hewstone, M., Glick, P., & Esses, V. M. (Eds.). (2010). *The Sage handbook of prejudice, stereotyping and discrimination*. Thousand Oaks, CA: Sage Publications.

11.5 Environmental Attitudes

Human behaviour has been producing unprecedented environmental transformations, and the cumulative impact of humanity on the planet is far greater than that of any other species. In order to address environmental problems, it is necessary to have a better understanding of the extent to which individuals hold particular attitudes that might lead them to form behavioural intentions to engage in pro-environmental behaviours. However, attitudes and behaviour concerning the environment differ from one culture to another to the extent that they are modulated by environmental variations, the resources available, and the societal context including values, regulations, infrastructure, and opportunities for action (e.g., Gifford & Sussman, 2012; Moser & Uzzell, 2003). Nevertheless, the study of attitudes towards the environment is indeed a key topic in the field of environmental psychology.

Environmental attitudes. The collection of beliefs, affects, and behavioural intentions a person holds regarding environmentally related activities or issues.

Environmental attitudes are defined in various ways. For example, according to Schultz et al. (2004, p. 31), environmental attitudes are "the collection of beliefs, affects, and behavioral intentions a person holds regarding environmentally related activities or issues." In turn, Hawcroft and Milfont (2010, p. 143) define them as "a psychological tendency expressed by evaluating the natural environment with some degree of favor or disfavor," while Gifford and Sussman (2012, p. 65) define them simply as "concern for the environment or caring about environmental issues." Therefore, what distinguishes environmental attitudes from attitudes in general is their object (broadly understood environment), and various general aspects of it (e.g., nature, climate, or cities) or a class of specific environmental issues or behaviours (e.g., recycling, saving energy and water, composting, or using individual vs. collective means of transportation).

The most commonly used scale for measuring general environmental attitudes is the **New Environmental Paradigm** (NEP) Scale (Dunlap et al., 2000). It measures people's concerns about global environmental issues, and therefore, the scale is useful in research on a wide variety of attitudes, from climate change to recycling. The NEP measures five facets of general environmental concern: (1) the reality of limits to growth, (2) anti-anthropocentrism, (3) the fragility of nature's balance, (4) rejection of exemptionalism, that is, the belief in the uniqueness of man, and (5) the possibility of an eco-crisis. Obviously, the predictive power of this scale for people's pro-environmental intentions and/or behaviours depends on the specific action. For example, when measuring behavioural intentions to engage in pro-environmental behaviours in general, scores on the NEP are a significant, although not the only, predictor (Cordano et al., 2003). However, for example, Kurtz et al.'s (2007) study found that general environmental concern had no significant effect on recycling programme participation, in contrast to more specific attitudes towards recycling. Also, in the study by Edgerton et al. (2008) on engagement in

New Environmental Paradigm (NEP). A set of beliefs and values that emphasises the interconnectedness of humans and the environment, recognises the intrinsic value of nature, acknowledges the limits of ecological systems, advocates for sustainable practices and a shift away from anthropocentric views.

home composting, it was found that general pro-environmental attitudes had no significant influence on it. One of the main reasons for these contradictory results, as with attitudes in general, is the specificity of individual pro-environmental behaviours. General attitudes may be a poor predictor of specific actions, as each has a unique set of underlying factors (including attitudes towards the behaviour). Nevertheless, general attitudes can influence trends or dispositions in many pro-environmental behaviours. The advantages and limitations of using the NEP in research are discussed in detail by Hawcroft and Milfont (2010).

Another approach to general, that is, object-independent, environmental attitudes, and especially their structure, is developed by Milfont and Duckitt (2004). Based on a thorough analysis of existing environmental attitude measures, they identified two distinct overarching dimensions: preservation (including pro-environmental behaviour) and utilisation (including economic liberalism and the idea that the environment needs to be preserved for human consumption). These dimensions reflect the fundamental conflict between preservation of natural resources on one hand and utilisation of natural resources on the other hand. Milfont and Duckitt (2010) also developed the Environmental Attitudes Inventory, which allows for the measurement of attitudes on these two dimensions and their 12 facets.

From the perspective of analysing the impact of pro-environmental attitudes on specific behaviours, the most commonly used model is the **TPB** (Ajzen, 1991), described in Section 4.3.1. In this model, pro-environmental behaviour is predicted by specific behavioural intentions, which are, in turn, predicted by attitudes, perceived social norms, and perceived behavioural control. This theory has been tested, among others, in the context of environmental behaviours including mobility behaviour (e.g., car use, park-and-ride, use of public transportation), waste behaviour (e.g., recycling, waste reduction, reuse), energy behaviour (e.g., energy saving, energy use), water use, green electricity, and green tourism. The results of a meta-analysis conducted by Klöckner (2013) confirmed the TPB. Generally, intentions to act, perceived behavioural control, and subjective norms were identified as predictors of both behavioural intention and the behaviour itself. This means that it is difficult, if not impossible, to predict, for example, the behaviour of someone with positive attitudes towards the protection of endangered animal species. Will they protest in front of fur shops, or simply refrain from buying them? Will they chain themselves to a tree in a nature reserve to prevent the construction of a highway? Will they only protect bird nests, or will they also relocate frogs migrating to their nesting grounds on the other side of the road? However, if we focus, as Ajzen (1991) suggests, on attitudes towards these specific behaviours, attitudes towards them may prove to be a very strong predictor.

Another important aspect of analysing various specific environmental attitudes is their interrelationship. Most studies clearly indicate that various pro-environmental attitudes are independent and based on different factors (e.g., McKenzie-Mohr, 2000). This means that a positive attitude towards recycling may be unrelated to water conservation, while both may be related to energy conservation. However, some studies are more optimistic and suggest that relationships between various environmental attitudes may exist. For example, Larsen (1995) found significant and strong correlations between attitudes towards recycling and attitudes towards the preservation of river salmon. Furthermore, environmental attitudes that predict individual behaviours (e.g., recycling) may also predict other similar behaviours. However, such a **spillover effect** occurs more often with behaviours associated with low rather than high effort (e.g., turning off lights after leaving a room vs. purchasing an energy-efficient car) (e.g., Henn et al., 2020).

Environmental attitudes are often linked to other attitudes and beliefs beyond this domain, especially political attitudes (see Chapter 2 on the inter-attitudinal structure). Numerous studies provide evidence that left-wing (liberal) individuals' attitudes towards climate change are significantly more strongly associated with preventive action, while right-wing (conservative) individuals often outright deny any climate change (e.g., McCright et al., 2016; Ziegler, 2017).

Besides being linked to political attitudes, environmental attitudes are also a component of religious belief systems. For example, fundamentalist Christians generally have lower levels of environmental concern than other groups (e.g., Schultz et al., 2000). This also appears to be significantly related to how the Bible is interpreted. Weak pro-environmental attitudes are more likely to develop when the Bible is interpreted as meaning that the earth and its resources were given to humans for use as desired. However, attitudes will be more

Spillover effect. Environmental attitudes that predict individual behaviours (e.g., recycling) may also predict other similar behaviours.

pro-environmental when the Bible's message is understood as meaning that humans are charged with caring for and preserving the earth.

In summary, analysing environmental attitudes is important because they often, though not always, determine behaviour that either increases or decreases environmental quality. Attitudes may predict specific behaviours (e.g., recycling or energy conservation), but they may also have some general predictive value. Research findings on environmental attitudes are also important in building public support for environmental action. However, they can be the basis for interventions and marketing campaigns aimed at changing people's behaviour to be more environmentally friendly (e.g., McKenzie-Mohr et al., 2012). Furthermore, the results of research on environmental attitudes can and do provide a basis for policymakers' decision-making and can help design educational programmes.

Further Reading

Gifford, R., & Sussman, R. (2012). Environmental attitudes. In S. D. Clayton (Ed.), *The Oxford handbook of environmental and conservation psychology* (pp. 65–80). Oxford: Oxford University Press.

References

Ajzen, I. (1991). The theory of planned behavior. *Organizational Behavior and Human Decision Processes*, *50*(2), 179–211.

Albarracín, D., & Johnson, B. T. (Eds.). (2018). *Handbook of attitudes, Volume 2: Applications*. New York: Routledge.

Albarracín, D., Jung, H., Song, W., Tan, A., & Fishman, J. (2021). Rather than inducing psychological reactance, requiring vaccination strengthens intentions to vaccinate in US populations. *Scientific Reports*, *11*(1), 20796.

Atkin, C., & Salmon, C. T. (2012). Persuasive strategies in health campaigns. In J. P. Dillard, & L. Shen (Eds.), *Persuasive strategies in health campaigns* (2nd ed., pp. 278–295). Thousand Oaks, CA: Sage Publications.

Bar-Tal, D., Hameiri, B., & Halperin, E. (2021). Paradoxical thinking as a paradigm of attitude change in the context of intractable conflict. In B. Gawronski (Ed.), *Advances in experimental social psychology* (Vol. 63, pp. 129–187). New York: Academic Press.

Betsch, C., & Böhm, R. (2016). Detrimental effects of introducing partial compulsory vaccination: Experimental evidence. *European Journal of Public health*, *26*(3), 378–381.

Blankenship, K. L., & Craig, T. Y. (2011). Language use and persuasion: Multiple roles for linguistic styles. *Social and Personality Psychology Compass*, *5*(4), 194–205.

Blankenship, K. L., & Holtgraves, T. (2005). The role of different markers of linguistic powerlessness in persuasion. *Journal of Language and Social Psychology*, *24*(1), 3–24.

Bohner, G., Einwiller, S., Erb, H. P., & Siebler, F. (2003). When small means comfortable: Relations between product attributes in two-sided advertising. *Journal of Consumer Psychology, 13*(4), 454–463.

Brader, T. (2005). Striking a responsive chord: How political ads motivate and persuade voters by appealing to emotions. *American Journal of Political Science, 49*(2), 388–405.

Brauer M. (2024). Stuck on intergroup attitudes: The need to shift gears to change intergroup behaviors. *Perspectives on Psychological Science, 19*(1), 280–294.

Brauer, M., Er-rafiy, A., Kawakami, K., & Phills, C. E. (2012). Describing a group in positive terms reduces prejudice less effectively than describing it in positive and negative terms. *Journal of Experimental Social Psychology, 48*(3), 757–761.

Brewer, P. R., & Gross, K. (2005). Values, framing, and citizens' thoughts about policy issues: Effects on content and quantity. *Political Psychology, 26*(6), 929–948.

Broyles, S. J. (2006). Subliminal advertising and the perpetual popularity of playing to people's paranoia. *The Journal of Consumer Affairs, 40*(2), 392–406.

Cacioppo, J. T., & Petty, R. E. (1985). Central and peripheral routes to persuasion: The role of message repetition. In L. Alwitt, & A. Mitchell (Eds.), *Psychological processes and advertising effects* (pp. 91–112). Hillsdale, NJ: Lawrence Erlbaum Associates.

Campbell, M. C. (1995). When attention-getting advertising tactics elicit consumer inferences of manipulative intent: The importance of balancing benefits and investments. *Journal of Consumer Psychology, 4*(3), 225–254.

Cho, C. H., & Cheon, H. J. (2004). Why do people avoid advertising on the internet? *Journal of Advertising, 33*(4), 89–97.

Chong, D., & Druckman, J. N. (2007). Framing theory. *Annual Review of Political Science, 10*, 103–126.

Claypool, H. M., Mackie, D. M., Garcia-Marques, T., McIntosh, A., & Udal, A. (2004). The effects of personal relevance and repetition on persuasive processing. *Social Cognition, 22*(3), 310–335.

Cohen, G. L. (2003). Party over policy: The dominating impact of group influence on political beliefs. *Journal of Personality and Social Psychology, 85*(5), 808–822.

Cohen, M. (2022). Cancer fatalism: Attitudes toward screening and care. In J. L. Steel, & B. I. Carr (Eds.), *Psychological aspects of cancer: A guide to emotional and psychological consequences of cancer, their causes, and their management* (2nd ed., pp. 301–318). Cham: Springer.

Cordano, M., Welcomer, S. A., & Scherer, R. F. (2003). An analysis of the predictive validity of the new ecological paradigm scale. *Journal of Environmental Education, 34*(3), 22–28.

Crawford, J. T., Kay, S. A., & Duke, K. E. (2015). Speaking out of both sides of their mouths: Biased political judgments within (and between) individuals. *Social Psychological and Personality Science, 6*(4), 422–430.

Cwalina, W., Falkowski, A., & Newman, B. I. (2015). Persuasion in the political context: Opportunities and threats. In D. W. Stewart (Ed.), *Handbook of persuasion and social marketing, Vol. 1: Historical and social foundations* (pp. 61–128). Santa Barbara, CA: Praeger.

Cwalina, W., & Koniak, P. (2023). The role of conspiracy mentality, reactance, and anxiety in the effectiveness of gain- vs. loss-framed messages promoting

COVID-19 protective measures: Is vaccination different? *Polish Psychological Bulletin, 54*(4), 279–288.
Cwalina, W., & Koniak, P. (2025a). Persuasion. In A. Nai, M. Grömping, & D. Wirz (Eds.), *Elgar encyclopedia of political communication*. Vol. 3, pp. 186–190. Cheltenham: Edward Elgar Publishing.
Cwalina, W., & Koniak, P. (2025b). Priming. In A. Nai, M. Grömping, & D. Wirz (Eds.), *Elgar encyclopedia of political communication*. Vol. 3, pp. 348–352. Cheltenham: Edward Elgar Publishing.
Djupe, P. A., & Calfano, B. R. (2013). Religious value priming, threat, and political tolerance. *Political Research Quarterly, 66*(4), 768–780.
Dovidio, J. F., Hewstone, M., Glick, P., & Esses, V. M. (Eds.). (2010). *The Sage handbook of prejudice, stereotyping and discrimination*. Thousand Oaks, CA: Sage Publications.
Dovidio, J. F., Schellhaas, F. M., & Pearson, A. R. (2018). The role of attitudes in intergroup relations. In D. Albarracín, & B. T. Johnson (Eds.), *Handbook of attitudes, Volume 2: Applications* (pp. 419–454). New York: Routledge.
Druckman, J. M., Jacobs, L. R., & Ostermeier, E. (2004). Candidate strategies to prime issues and image. *Journal of Politics, 66*(4), 1180–1202.
Druckman, J. N. (2001). On the limits of framing effects: Who can frame? *Journal of Politics, 63*(4), 1041–1066.
Dunlap, R. E., Van Liere, K. D., Mertig, A. G., & Jones, R. E. (2000). Measuring endorsement of the new ecological paradigm: A revised NEP scale. *Journal of Social Issues, 56*(3), 425–442.
Edgerton, E., McKechnie, J., & Dunleavy, K. (2008). Behavioral determinants of household participation in a home composting scheme. *Environment and Behavior, 41*(2), 151–169.
Esses, V. M. (2021). Prejudice and discrimination toward immigrants. *Annual Review of Psychology, 72*, 503–531.
Fennis, B. M., & Stroebe, W. (2010). *The psychology of advertising*. London: Psychology Press.
Gifford, R., & Sussman, R. (2012). Environmental attitudes. In S. D. Clayton (Ed.), *The Oxford handbook of environmental and conservation psychology* (pp. 65–80). Oxford: Oxford University Press.
Hameiri, B., Porat, R., Bar-Tal, D., Bieler, A., & Halperin, E. (2014). Paradoxical thinking as a new avenue of intervention to promote peace. *PNAS Proceedings of the National Academy of Sciences of the United States of America, 111*(30), 10996–11001.
Hauser, D. J., & Schwarz, N. (2015). The war on prevention: Bellicose cancer metaphors hurt (some) prevention intentions. *Personality & Social Psychology Bulletin, 41*(1), 66–77.
Hauser, D. J., & Schwarz, N. (2020). The war on prevention II: Battle metaphors undermine cancer treatment and prevention and do not increase vigilance. *Health Communication, 35*(13), 1698–1704.
Hawcroft, L. J., & Milfont, T. L. (2010). The use (and abuse) of the new environmental paradigm scale over the last 30 years: A meta-analysis. *Journal of Environmental Psychology, 30*(2), 143–158.
Heath, R., Brandt, D., & Nairn, A. (2006). Brand relationships: Strengthened by emotion, weakened by attention. *Journal of Advertising Research, 46*(4), 410–419.

Henn, L., Otto, S., & Kaiser, F. G. (2020). Positive spillover: The result of attitude change. *Journal of Environmental Psychology, 69*, 101429.

Hosman, L. A., & Siltanen, S. A. (2006). Powerful and powerless language forms: Their consequences for impression formation, attributions of control of self and control of others, cognitive responses, and message memory. *Journal of Language and Social Psychology, 25*(1), 33–46.

Iyengar, S., & Kinder, D. R. (1987). *News that matters: Television and American opinion*. Chicago, IL: University of Chicago Press.

Iyengar, S., Sood, G., & Lelkes, Y. (2012). Affect, not ideology: A social identity perspective on polarization. *Public Opinion Quarterly, 76*(3), 405–431.

Iyengar, S., & Westwood, S. J. (2015). Fear and loathing across party lines: New evidence on group polarization. *American Journal of Political Science, 59*(3), 690–707.

Janssen, L., & Fennis, B. M. (2017). Mindless resistance to persuasion: Low self-control fosters the use of resistance-promoting heuristics. *Journal of Consumer Behaviour, 16*(6), 536–549.

Johnson, J. D., Olivo, N., Gibson, N., Reed, W., & Ashburn-Nardo, L. (2009). Priming media stereotypes reduces support for social welfare policies: The mediating role of empathy. *Personality and Social Psychology Bulletin, 35*(4), 463–476.

Jussim, L., Crawford, J. T., & Rubinstein, R. S. (2015). Stereotype (in)accuracy in perceptions of groups and individuals. *Current Directions in Psychological Science, 24*(6), 490–497.

Karremans, J. C., Stroebe, W., & Claus, J. (2006). Beyond Vicary's fantasies: The impact of subliminal priming and brand choice. *Journal of Experimental Social Psychology, 42*(6), 792–798.

Klöckner, C. A. (2013). A comprehensive model of the psychology of environmental behaviour – A meta-analysis. *Global Environmental Change, 23*(5), 1028–138.

Koniak, P., & Cwalina, W. (2020). Fear of coronavirus and forbid/allow asymmetry as determinants of acceptance of COVID-19 pandemic related restrictions and persistence of attitudes towards these regulations. *Social Psychological Bulletin, 15*(4), Article e4421.

Koniak, P., & Cwalina, W. (2025). When fear meets anger: Attitudes toward positively versus negatively evaluated pandemic policy proposals when negative emotions are competing in society. *Analyses of Social Issues and Public Policy, 25*(2), e70015.

Kriss, L. A., Quick, B. L., Rains, S. A., & Barbati, J. L. (2022). Psychological reactance theory and COVID-19 vaccine mandates: The roles of threat magnitude and direction of threat. *Journal of Health Communication, 27*(9), 654–663.

Kurtz, T., Linden, M., & Sheehy, N. (2007). Attitudinal and community influences on participation in new curbside recycling initiatives in Northern Ireland. *Environment and Behavior, 39*(3), 367–391.

Larsen, K. S. (1995). Environmental waste: Recycling attitudes and correlates. *Journal of Social Psychology, 135*(1), 83–88.

Levendusky, M. (2018). Americans, not partisans: Can priming American national identity reduce affective polarization? *Journal of Politics, 80*(1), 59–70.

Leventhal, H., Cameron, L., Leventhal, E. A., & Ozakinci, G. (2005). Do messages from your body, your friends, your doctor, or the media shape your health behavior? In T. C. Brock, & M. C. Green (Eds.), *Persuasion: Psychological insights and perspectives* (2nd ed., pp. 195–223). Thousand Oaks, CA: Sage Publications.

Maddux, J. E., & Rogers, R. W. (1983). Protection motivation and self-efficacy: A revised theory of fear appeals and attitude change. *Journal of Experimental Social Psychology, 19*(5), 469–479.

Maheswaran, D., & Meyers-Levy, J. (1990). The influence of message framing and issue involvement. *Journal of Marketing Research, 27*(3), 361–367.

Marcus, G. E., & Mackuen, M. B. (1993). Anxiety, enthusiasm, and the vote: The emotional underpinnings of learning and involvement during presidential campaigns. *American Political Science Review, 87*(3), 672–685.

McCright, A. M., Dunlap, R. E., & Marquart-Pyatt, S. T. (2016). Political ideology and views about climate change in the European Union. *Environmental Politics, 25*(2), 338–358.

McKenzie-Mohr, D. (2000). Promoting sustainable behavior: An introduction to community-based social marketing. *Journal of Social Issues, 56*(3), 543–554.

McKenzie-Mohr, D., Lee, N. R., Schultz, P. W., & Kotler, P. (2012). *Social marketing to protect the environment: What works.* Thousand Oaks, CA: Sage Publications.

Meyers-Levy, J., & Maheswaran, D. (2004). Exploring message framing outcomes when systematic, heuristic, or both types of processing occur. *Journal of Consumer Psychology, 14*(1–2), 159–167.

Milfont, T. L., & Duckitt, J. (2004). The structure of environmental attitudes: A first- and second-order confirmatory factor analysis. *Journal of Environmental Psychology, 24*(3), 289–303.

Milfont, T. L., & Duckitt, J. (2010). The environmental attitudes inventory: A valid and reliable measure to assess the structure of environmental attitudes. *Journal of Environmental Psychology, 30*(1), 80–94.

Mongeau, P. (2012). Fear appeals. In J. P. Dillard, & L. Shen (Eds.), *The Sage handbook of persuasion: Developments in theory and practice* (2nd ed., pp. 184–199). Thousand Oaks, CA: Sage Publications.

Moons, W. G., Mackie, D. M., & Garcia-Marques, T. (2009). The impact of repetition-induced familiarity on agreement with weak and strong arguments. *Journal of Personality and Social Psychology, 96*(1), 32–44.

Moser, G., & Uzzell, D. L. (2003). Environmental psychology. In T. Millon, & M. J. Lerner (Eds.), *Comprehensive handbook of psychology, Volume 5: Personality and social psychology* (pp. 419–445). New York: John Wiley & Sons.

Mullinix, K. J., & Lythgoe, T. (2023). Priming norms to combat affective polarization. *Political Research Quarterly, 76*(1), 186–199.

Nelson, T. E., Oxley, Z. M., & Clawson, R. A. (1997). Toward a psychology of framing effects. *Political Behavior, 19*(3), 221–246.

O'Keefe, D. J., & Jensen, J. D. (2007). The relative persuasiveness of gain-framed loss-framed messages for encouraging disease prevention behaviors: A meta-analytic review. *Journal of Health Communication, 12*(7), 623–644.

O'Keefe, D. J., & Jensen, J. D. (2009). The relative persuasiveness of gain-framed and loss-framed messages for encouraging disease detection behaviors: A meta-analytic review. *Journal of Communication, 59*(2), 296–316.

O'Keefe, D. J., & Nan, X. (2012). The relative persuasiveness of gain- and loss-framed messages for promoting vaccination: A meta-analytic review. *Health Communication, 27*(8), 776–783.

Paluck, E. L., & Green, D. P. (2009). Prejudice reduction: What works? A review and assessment of research and practice. *Annual Review of Psychology, 60*, 339–367.

Paluck, E. L., Porat, R., Clark, C. S., & Green, D. P. (2021). Prejudice reduction: Progress and challenges. *Annual Review of Psychology, 72*, 533–560.

Priester, J. R., Nayakankuppam, D., Fleming, M. A., & Godek, J. (2004). The A^2SC^2 Model: The influence of attitudes and attitude strength on consideration and choice. *Journal of Consumer Research, 30*(4), 574–587.

Rothman, A. J., & Salovey, P. (1997). Shaping perceptions to motivate healthy behavior: The role of message framing. *Psychological Bulletin, 121*(1), 3–19.

Rothman, A. J., & Salovey, P. (2007). The reciprocal relation between principles and practice: Social psychology and health behavior. In A. W. Kruglanski, & E. T. Higgins (Eds.), *Social psychology: Handbook of basic principles* (2nd ed., pp. 826–849). New York: Guilford Press.

Ruiter, R. A., Kessels, L. T., Peters, G. J., & Kok, G. (2014). Sixty years of fear appeal research: Current state of the evidence. *International Journal of Psychology, 49*(2), 63–70.

Santoso, I., Wright, M., Trinh, G., & Avis, M. (2020). Is digital advertising effective under conditions of low attention? *Journal of Marketing Management, 36*(17–18), 1707–1730.

Schmid, P., Böhm, R., Das, E., Holford, D., Korn, L., Leask, J., Lewandowsky, S., Shapiro, G. K., Sprengholz, P., & Betsch, C. (2024). Vaccination mandates and their alternatives and complements. *Nature Reviews Psychology, 3*(12), 789–803.

Schmidt, S., & Eisend, M. (2015). Advertising repetition: A meta-analysis on effective frequency in advertising. *Journal of Advertising, 44*(4), 415–428.

Schultz, P. W., Shriver, C., Tabanico, J. J., & Khazian, A. M. (2004). Implicit connections with nature. *Journal of Environmental Psychology, 24*(1), 31–42.

Schultz, P. W., Zelezny, L., & Dalrymple, N. J. (2000). A multinational perspective on the relation between Judeo-Christian religious beliefs and attitudes of environmental concern. *Environment and Behavior, 32*(4), 576–591.

Shen, L., & Dillard, J. P. (2014). Threat, fear, and persuasion: Review and critique of questions about functional form. *Review of Communication Research, 2*, 94–114.

Simon, A. F., & Jerit, J. (2007). Toward a theory relating political discourse, media, and public opinion. *Journal of Communication, 57*(2), 254–271.

Smarandescu, L., & Shimp, T. A. (2015). Drink Coca-Cola, eat popcorn, and choose Powerade: Testing the limits of subliminal persuasion. *Marketing Letters, 26*(4), 715–726.

Strahan, E. J., Spencer, S. J., & Zanna, M. P. (2002). Subliminal priming and persuasion: Striking while the iron is hot. *Journal of Experimental Social Psychology, 38*(6), 556–568.

Sweeny, K., & Rankin, K. (2018). The role of attitudes in cancer. In D. Albarracín, & B. T. Johnson (Eds.), *Handbook of attitudes, Volume 2: Applications* (pp. 3–30). New York: Routledge.

Tajfel, H., & Turner, J. C. (1979). An integrative theory of intergroup conflict. In W. G. Austin, & S. Worchel (Eds.), *The social psychology of intergroup relations* (pp. 33–37). Monterey, CA: Brooks/Cole.

Tannenbaum, M. B., Hepler, J., Zimmerman, R. S., Saul, L., Jacobs, S., Wilson, K., & Albarracín, D. (2015). Appealing to fear: A meta-analysis of fear appeal effectiveness and theories. *Psychological Bulletin, 141*(6), 1178–1204.

Witte, K. (1992). Putting the fear back into fear appeals: The extended parallel process model. *Communication Monographs, 59*(4), 329–349.

Witte, K., & Allen, M. (2000). A meta-analysis of fear appeals: implications for effective public health campaigns. *Health Education & Behavior, 27*(5), 591–615.

Wojcieszak, M., & Garrett, R. K. (2018). Social identity, selective exposure, and affective polarization: How priming national identity shapes attitudes toward immigrants via news selection. *Human Communication Research, 44*(3), 247–273.

Yaqub, O., Castle-Clarke, S., Sevdalis, N., & Chataway, J. (2014). Attitudes to vaccination: A critical review. *Social Science & Medicine (1982), 112*, 1–11.

Ziegler, A. (2017). Political orientation, environmental values, and climate change beliefs and attitudes: An empirical cross country analysis. *Energy Economics, 63*, 144–153.

Part 5

Key Emerging Areas

This section in summary

- Personalised persuasion and theories explaining the consequences of tailoring messages to the individual characteristics or induced states of the recipients
- The role of cultural differences in persuasion
- Polarising consequences of selective exposure, and ways to increase openness to opposing viewpoints and depolarisation of attitudes
- Role of psychological inoculation and persuasion knowledge in preventing malevolent persuasion

DOI: 10.4324/9781003589174-16

Chapter 12

Changing Attitudes in a Globalised World

12.1 Attitudes and Persuasion in Times of Tailored Messages

The key to persuasion through mass communication lies in creating effective messages **tailored** to specific groups of people. These messages may vary according to the presumed characteristics of the recipients. Technological progress and internet tools have recently made it possible to identify the characteristics of every potential recipient of a message. These characteristics can be as obvious as gender or age – information that is often revealed by social media users themselves – or as subtle and less visible as personality traits. For example, Kosinski and his colleagues (2013) could predict sensitive personal attributes such as sexual orientation, ethnicity, religious and political views, personality traits, intelligence, happiness, substance abuse, parental separation, age, and gender based on a person's Facebook likes. Armed with such precise knowledge, persuaders can create personalised messages and situations for each individual recipient. Indeed, each person – or at least each group – can receive different messages designed to persuade them to do the same thing. Every element of persuasive communication can be tailored to the recipient's characteristics, including the source, the message, and the context.

This process is known as **personalised persuasion** (Petty et al., 2025), though it is often referred to as tailoring, matching, or targeting in the literature.

Personalised persuasion (also tailoring, matching, targeting). Persuasive communication tailored to the recipient's characteristics.

12.1.1 Functional Matching

As the functional approach to attitudes (see Section 2.2) suggests, people's attitudes towards the same object can serve different functions. According to

DOI: 10.4324/9781003589174-17

the **matching hypothesis** (see Joyal-Desmarais et al., 2025, for further discussion), people are more likely to be persuaded if the attempt to persuade them matches the underlying function of their attitude. For example, some people's attitudes primarily serve a social-adjustive function, while the attitudes of others primarily serve a value-expressive function. The **Self-Monitoring** Scale (Snyder & Gangestad, 1986) can be used to measure this tendency. People who score highly on the Self-Monitoring Scale desire to fit into the social situations they are in. They try to obtain a desired public appearance and regulate their self-presentation to achieve this. In contrast, those who score low on the Self-Monitoring Scale lack the ability or motivation to regulate their self-presentation. Instead, their behaviour is guided by the desire to express their personal values, attitudes, or emotional state.

Matching hypothesis. Hypothesis that people are more likely to be persuaded if the attempt to persuade them matches the underlying function of their attitude.

Self-Monitoring. A relatively stable trait related to the ability to adapt one's behaviour in response to social situations.

Thus, the attitudes of individuals with high self-monitoring tendencies primarily serve a social-adjustive function, whereas those of individuals with low self-monitoring tendencies primarily serve a value-expressive function. Consequently, high self-monitors are more persuaded by advertisements that focus on a product's image-related benefits than on its quality. The reverse is true for low self-monitors (Snyder & DeBono, 1985). This effect is mediated by subjective **perceptions of message quality**. Lavine and Snyder (1996) demonstrated this using a pro-turnout campaign. High self-monitors perceived the social-adjustive message (e.g., that a majority of their peers planned to vote in an upcoming election and that voting could enhance their status, popularity, and attractiveness) as higher quality than the functionally mismatched value-expressive message (e.g., that voting allows them to express their support for values such as freedom, liberty, and democracy, and that by voting they can act on their own attitudes and beliefs about the issues and candidates). Conversely, low self-monitors perceived the functionally matched value-expressive message as higher quality than the social-adjustive message, which was functionally mismatched for them.

Functional matching can also affect the **level of elaboration**. Messages that align with the functional basis of attitudes tend to be processed more extensively than those that do not. This effect is particularly evident among people with a low need for cognition – that is to say, people who do not usually process messages extensively. However, it should be remembered that increased processing of matching messages can make them more persuasive if they contain strong arguments; conversely, weak arguments can reduce their effectiveness (Petty & Wegener, 1998).

The message is not the only aspect of a persuasive situation that can be matched or mismatched with the attitude function. For example, the **source** may also be consequential. If high self-monitoring receivers are primarily concerned about social adjustment, they should be particularly interested in what attractive sources have to say. Conversely, low self-monitoring receivers, who are primarily concerned with the alignment of their attitude with their values, should find an expert a more compelling source of information. In fact, research by DeBono and Harnish (1988) confirmed that high self-monitoring people tend to process messages from attractive sources systematically, whereas those from expert sources are processed rather heuristically. Conversely, low self-monitoring individuals process messages from expert sources systematically and messages from attractive sources heuristically.

12.1.2 Regulatory Fit Theory

According to regulatory fit theory (Higgins, 2005), people with specific motivational orientations prefer particular means of pursuing goals. When they use these preferred means, they experience a state called **regulatory fit**. This has two consequences. First, a person experiencing regulatory fit feels right about what they are doing. Second, they become more engaged in the activity of pursuing the goal.

Research within this theory primarily focuses on particular instances of motivational orientation, as outlined in **regulatory focus theory** (Higgins, 1998). According to this theory, there are two self-regulatory systems: a promotion focus and a prevention focus. People with a **promotion focus** concentrate on achieving their goals, hopes, and aspirations. They are sensitive to positive outcomes and concerned with accomplishment and advancement, considering missing an opportunity worse than making a mistake. In contrast,

Regulatory fit. A state experienced by people with specific motivational orientations when pursuing their goals in their preferred way.

Promotion focus. A motivational orientation towards achieving goals, hopes, and aspirations, characterised by sensitivity to positive outcomes, a focus on accomplishment and advancement, and a preference for eager strategic means.

those with a **prevention focus** concentrate on avoiding losses and on their duties and obligations. They are sensitive to negative outcomes and concerned with safety and security, considering avoiding errors to be more important than missing opportunities. Therefore, individuals with a promotion focus prefer eager strategic means, while individuals with a prevention focus prefer vigilant strategic means.

> **Prevention focus.** A motivational orientation towards fulfilling duties and obligations, characterised by sensitivity to negative outcomes and avoidance of losses, concerns with safety and security, and a preference for vigilant strategic means.

All of this has important consequences for the persuasion process. Overall, Cesario and his collaborators (2008) proposed several mechanisms that influence the effectiveness of regulatory fitted versus non-fitted communication (see Lee, 2025, for a wider discussion). First, receivers feeling right about the message may use this feeling as information in inferring their attitude towards the object of persuasion. Furthermore, regulatory fit may increase the receiver's confidence in their evaluation of the object. Moreover, it may make those recipients feel right about their reactions to the message. Avnet and colleagues (2013) proposed that the operating mechanism depends on the receiver's involvement with the object of the attitude. When people are **highly involved**, fit increases reliance on evaluative reactions to the object of persuasion. Consequently, when these reactions are positive, regulatory fit increases attitudes, but when reactions are negative, regulatory fit lowers attitudes. However, **when involvement is low**, fit simply increases positivity towards the object of persuasion. This happens regardless of the direction of the message. Consequently, regulatory fit may backfire when the intention is to dissuade people from doing something. Trying to persuade uninvolved participants who experience fit that the object is bad may actually make them more positive towards it.

Regulatory fit may also increase engagement in message processing, resulting in the message being perceived as easier to process. Thus, it may also influence elaboration likelihood. However, the effect of regulatory fit on message processing appears to depend on how it is induced.

12.1.2.1 Integral Regulatory Fit Manipulations

Regulatory fit (or non-fit) may result from the relationship between the receiver's regulatory focus and elements of persuasive communication, like framing of arguments, even when the content of the argumentation remains exactly the same. For example, people with a promotion focus

Integral regulatory fit. Regulatory fit induced by elements of persuasive communication.

were more persuaded by the introduction of a new city tax for an after-school programme for children when the programme was presented using **eager means framing** ("it will advance children's education and support more children to succeed") than when it was presented with **vigilant means framing** ("it will secure children's education and prevent more children from failing"). The reverse was true for promotion-focused participants (Cesario et al., 2004).

Moreover, when receivers generate mostly negative message-related thoughts, such regulatory fit leads to reduced persuasion, as the fit itself increases the perceived "rightness" of one's evaluations, whether positive or negative. Furthermore, directing people's attention to the correct source of their feeling right (e.g., by asking how much they "feel right" about pursuing their goal) eliminates this effect and decreases people's confidence in their attitudes. This confirms that the persuasive effect of regulatory fit is based on people **misattributing** their feeling-right experience to their persuasion-related activity. This is an important point, as this feeling right may result from non-essential changes in the wording of arguments or even the non-verbal behaviour of the source. Cesario and Higgins (2008) demonstrated that a speaker displaying **non-verbal eagerness** (e.g., animated gestures, leaning forward and a fast speech, and body movement rate) is more persuasive when addressing promotion-focused receivers. Conversely, a speaker displaying **non-verbal signs of vigilance** (e.g., precise gestures, leaning back and a slower speech, and body movement rate) is more persuasive when addressing prevention-focused receivers. Regulatory fit may also be affected by the visual or stylistic elements of an advertising message. For example, promotion-focused receivers experience more regulatory fit (and evaluate the product more positively) when the product is **photographed from the actor's perspective**. However, when the **observer's perspective** is used, regulatory fit occurs (and the positive evaluation of the product increases) among those who are prevention-focused (Zhang & Yang, 2015).

Finally, some results suggest that regulatory fit stemming from **integral regulatory fit** manipulation – that is, when induced by elements of persuasive communication, such as the source or argumentation – **increases message processing**. This results in receivers experiencing regulatory fit generating more thoughts related to the merit of the persuasion (Cesario et al., 2004).

12.1.2.2 Incidental Regulatory Fit Manipulations

Feelings of rightness or wrongness resulting from regulatory fit or non-fit may also come from **incidental sources** outside of persuasive communication. These feelings may be evoked by an **unrelated previous situation** and still influence reactions to a subsequent persuasive message. This case is called **incidental regulatory fit**. For example, promotion-focused individuals experience fit when asked to describe eager ways of achieving a goal. However, when asked about vigilant ways, they experience a sense of non-fit. Consequently, when an unrelated persuasive message is presented later, those with induced incidental fit have a more positive attitude towards the topic of persuasion than those with induced incidental non-fit (Cesario et al., 2004).

Incidental regulatory fit. Regulatory fit resulting from incidental sources outside of persuasive communication, for example, an unrelated previous situation.

Moreover, the incidental induction of fit or non-fit also affects the processing of persuasive appeals. Overall, unlike fit resulting from integral parts of persuasive communication, incidentally induced fit **decreases processing**. After incidental induction of fit, people rely more on peripheral cues, such as the expertise of the source, and become less sensitive to the strength of arguments and less resistant to changes in attitude. However, those with incidentally induced non-fit rely less on source characteristics, their attitudes are related to the quality of the argument, and they are more resistant to change (Koenig et al., 2009).

However, it should be noted that the effect may differ when an incidental regulatory fit is induced before reading a **narrative text** rather than before rhetorical persuasion. Specifically, when reading an unrelated story, individuals who experienced an incidentally induced regulatory fit reported greater emotional engagement than those who experienced an induced regulatory non-fit (Vaughn et al., 2009). Therefore, it appears that experiencing an incidental regulatory fit prior to reading narrative stories **enhances engagement with the story**.

12.1.3 Matching to Affective and Cognitive Bases of Attitudes

Attitudes towards different objects can be based primarily on affect (how a person feels about it) or cognition (what they believe about it; see Chapter 1). Similarly, persuasive communication may be predominantly affective or predominantly cognitive. The results of initial studies on matching persuasion to the affective or cognitive bases of attitudes were mixed. However, these results are complicated by methodological issues and differences between the studies (see Aquino et al., 2025; Fabrigar & Petty, 1999, for analyses of these studies and their methodologies). For this reason, Fabrigar and Petty (1999) conducted more controlled research. In one of their studies, they presented a positive description of a fictional animal called the "lemphur." To create affective attitudes, they presented an emotion-evoking set of information designed to produce positive feelings towards the object of the attitude. Cognitive-based attitudes were created by presenting information in the form of an encyclopaedia excerpt discussing the lemphur's positive attributes. Next, the participants' attitudes were modified using either affective messages that elicited negative emotions towards lemphurs, or cognitive messages in the form of an encyclopaedia excerpt describing negative lemphur attributes. The study found a **relative affective/cognitive persuasion matching effect**. An affective message was more effective at changing affect-based attitudes than cognition-based ones. However, there is no strong evidence that cognitive persuasion is more effective for cognitive than affective attitudes.

12.1.4 Matching to Situation Induced States and to Object of Persuasion

All of the above variables can be considered stable, individual characteristics that distinguish one person from another and that can be measured. However, they can also be influenced by situational factors and induced, at least temporarily. For example, Julka and Marsh (2000) demonstrated that the cognitive function of attitudes could be elicited by presenting participants with the methodology, findings, and discussion of scientific studies. Conversely, the value-expressive function can be induced by prompting participants to consider their values, for example, by asking them to complete a questionnaire. Furthermore, an unrelated advertisement presented subsequently was found to be more persuasive when it matched the induced attitude function. Similarly, many studies on regulatory fit have used induction rather than measurement of regulatory focus. One way to induce a prevention focus is to ask participants to think and write about their duties and obligations. To induce a promotion focus, participants are asked about their hopes and aspirations (Cesario et al., 2004).

It is important to note that matched messages may be more persuasive if the characteristics of the target audience are manipulated rather than measured or inferred (Joyal-Desmarais et al., 2022). This offers a different perspective on persuasion. Rather than assessing which characteristics to match, it may be easier and more effective to induce a specific orientation or motivation in order to prepare the ground for receptiveness to an incoming message.

In addition to the individual's assessed or induced state, the **attitude object** also plays a role, as persuasive communication can be matched or mismatched to it. Shavitt (1990) demonstrated that certain objects are predominantly associated with a single attitude function. For example, the attitude towards coffee serves a primarily utilitarian function, while the attitude towards perfume serves a primarily social identity function. Consequently, advertising utilitarian products is more effective when utilitarian arguments are used (e.g., the taste of the coffee) than social identity arguments (e.g., the coffee you drink reveals your personality). The reverse is true for social identity products. However, products are usually branded. **Branding** alters the associations between products and attitude functions. Attitudes towards branded utilitarian products become more symbolic than those towards non-branded products. Similarly, attitudes towards branded symbolic products become more utilitarian and less symbolic. Furthermore, while persuasive messages are more effective when matched to the function of non-branded products, this advantage disappears in the case of branded products (LeBoeuf & Simmons, 2010). When it comes to branded products, the message should probably be tailored to the specific functions of the brand rather than the category of the product.

Different **topics** in the message may also induce different regulatory orientations. Cesario et al. (2013) demonstrated that health messages concerning the consequences of sun exposure and addressing safety concerns such as skin cancer prompted a prevention mindset in recipients. However, when the message addressed concerns about growth or nurturance (e.g., wrinkles), a promotion focus was induced.

Further Reading

Petty, R. E., Luttrell, A., & Teeny, J. D. (Eds.). (2025). *The handbook of personalized persuasion: Theory and application.* New York: Routledge.

12.2 Attitudes and Persuasion in Globalised World

Globalisation processes have broadened the scope of persuasive attempts from the relatively monocultural to the multicultural. The same persuasive message can now reach people in different parts of the world, including countries with different cultures. Even within the same country, populations can be more or less culturally diverse. This raises questions about the role of sociocultural context in attitude formation and change. This issue is becoming increasingly important, given that most research into attitudes and persuasion has so far been conducted in a Western cultural context (Albarracin & Shavitt, 2018). For instance, individuals from Western cultures tend to view ambivalence negatively. Consequently, North Americans with ambivalent attitudes are more likely to change them in line with a persuasive message than those with unambivalent attitudes. However, people from East exhibit **tolerance**

for inconsistencies and contradictions. Among East Asians, attitude ambivalence was not associated with the degree of attitude change (Ng et al., 2012).

> **Cultural tailoring**. Communication adapted to the deep structures of the receiver's culture, such as values, traditions, and norms.
>
> **Surface tailoring**. Communication incorporating only superficial features of a given culture, such as language, appearance, or diet.

Overall, the cultural background of the recipient should be considered when attempting to persuade them (see Section 12.1). This directs researchers' attention towards cultural differences that may influence the formation of attitudes and the effectiveness of persuasion. Studies have shown that **culturally tailored** health communication, that is, communication that integrates a culture's deep structures (e.g., values, traditions, and norms), is more persuasive than communication based on **surface tailoring** (e.g., language or appearance; Huang & Shen, 2016). However, advertisements adapted to important cultural values (primarily the individualism-collectivism dimension) are overall only slightly more persuasive than unadapted or mismatched versions (Hornikx & O'Keefe, 2009). Below, we highlight examples of attitudinally and persuasively consequential cultural dimensions (see Shavitt, 2025, for a broader discussion).

12.2.1 *Individualism and Collectivism*

In this context, the most widely studied characteristic is the difference between cultures with individualistic and collectivist backgrounds and orientations. In **individualistic cultures** (e.g., North America and Europe), people tend to prioritise their own goals over the goals of the group. By contrast, people in **collectivist cultures** (e.g., China, Brazil, South Korea, and India) prioritise group goals over personal ones. They are also motivated to pursue harmony in their relationships (Shavitt, 2025). Han and Shavitt (1994) found that people from individualistic cultures (such as the United States) were more persuaded by ads **emphasising individual benefits** ("you will love it"), whereas those from collectivistic cultures (such as North Korea) were more persuaded by ads **emphasising family or group benefits** ("your family will love it"). However, Aaker and Williams (1998) demonstrated that messages evoking **ego-focused emotions** (such as pride or happiness) were more persuasive in collectivist cultures (such as China) than in individualist cultures (such as the United States), and the reverse was true for messages evoking **other-focused emotions** (such as empathy or peacefulness). This effect was based on the generation and elaboration of a relatively novel type of thought (individual-focused thoughts for collectivists and collective-focused thoughts for individualists), induced by a culturally mismatched emotional message. Therefore, it may be a specific case of overly surprising mismatching, causing a switch from an emotional reaction to thoughts.

Cultural specificity may also alter the role of certain variables in the persuasion process. Aaker and Maheswaran (1997) found that, even when highly motivated, members of collectivist cultures were influenced by seemingly heuristic cues, such as **consensus information** ("81% of consumers were extremely satisfied"). Furthermore, when this consensus information was incongruent with the product's attributes, individuals with low motivation based their attitudes on the consensus information rather than the product's attributes. By contrast, other studies have shown that people from individualistic cultures rely more on product attributes in such cases, as the perceived incongruence motivates them to process information more systematically. However, this was not because people from collectivist cultures engaged in a different processing pattern; rather, it was the consequence of the **cue's diagnosticity**. For members of collectivist cultures, information about consensus is not a heuristic cue but rather centrally relevant information. Consequently, they process it systematically, even when highly motivated. When a non-diagnostic cue (the number of arguments) was used, it only affected low-motivated individuals. Highly motivated individuals mostly based their attitudes on the quality of the arguments. These results replicated those found in individualist cultures.

The distinction between an independent ("I") and an interdependent ("we") self-construal relates to individualism and collectivism. Those with an **independent self-construal** view themselves as unique individuals, separate, and distinct from others, and define themselves by their individual characteristics. In contrast, those with an **interdependent self-construal** see themselves as part of a social context, connected to others and defined by their social relationships (Hong & Chang, 2015). While self-construal can be influenced by the situation, it is also shaped by culture. People from Western cultures tend to have an independent self-construal, whereas those from Eastern cultures tend to have an interdependent one. Aaker and Lee (2001) demonstrated that individuals with an accessible independent self-view are more receptive to **promotion-focused information** (e.g., the benefits of drinking purple grape juice for energy production). However, individuals with a more accessible interdependent self-view are more persuaded by **prevention-focused information** (e.g., the role of drinking juice in preventing cancer and heart disease). Moreover, such matched messages were processed more extensively. Hong and Chang (2015) provided evidence that an accessible independent self-construal increases reliance on feelings, whereas an accessible interdependent self-construal increases reliance on reasons. Furthermore, incidental moods influence judgements more among people with an independent self-construal than among those with an interdependent one. However, a meta-analysis focusing solely on persuasive appeals revealed that **affective appeals** are more effective than cognitive ones in collectivist cultures. In individualistic cultures, however, affective and cognitive appeals were found to be equally effective (Ng et al., 2025).

12.2.2 Horizontal and Vertical Cultures

Cultures may also differ in the emphasis they place on hierarchy. Shavitt with collaborators (2011) suggest that people in **vertical individualist societies** (such as the United States, Great Britain, and France) prioritise improving their personal status, viewing competition as a means of setting themselves apart from others. In contrast, people from **horizontal individualist societies** (e.g., Sweden, Denmark, and Australia) see themselves as equal to others and prioritise expressing their uniqueness and self-reliance. Those from **vertical collectivist societies** (e.g., East Asia, India, and Eastern Europe) tend to comply with authority, focusing on enhancing the cohesion and status of their ingroups. Finally, people from **horizontal collectivist societies** (e.g., Israeli kibbutzim) are egalitarian and prioritise sociability and interdependence with others. These cultural differences are reflected in the persuasive tactics used in advertising. Shavitt et al. (2011) found that advertising in vertical societies (including both individualist societies, such as the United States, and collectivist societies, such as Korea, Russia, and Poland) emphasised status more than advertising in horizontal individualist societies (such as Denmark). Advertisements focusing on uniqueness, such as depictions of differentiation, self-expression, self-reliance, and novelty, were more prevalent in horizontal individualist societies than in vertical societies.

The concept of **power distance** is related to this. It refers to the degree to which people in a given culture expect and accept differences in power (Shavitt, 2025). Consumers with higher power distance beliefs evaluate advertisements featuring **celebrities** more positively than those featuring non-celebrities, and they have a more positive attitude towards the brand when the message is celebrity-based. However, the status of the endorser is irrelevant to people with lower power distance beliefs (Winterich et al., 2018).

Further Reading

Shavitt, S. (2025). Culture and personalized persuasion. In R. E. Petty, A. Luttrell, & J. D. Teeny (Eds.), *The handbook of personalized persuasion: Theory and application* (pp. 165–190). New York: Routledge.

12.3 Attitudes and Persuasion in Times of Echo Chambers

The tendency of people to avoid information that challenges their point of view, and to prefer information that aligns with their beliefs, is nothing new (see Section 4.2). However, technological changes, as well as changes to the media landscape overall, have increased concerns about the tendency to isolate citizens in **echo chambers**. This refers to situations or media environments in which only ideas, information, beliefs, and attitudes that align with the user's point of view are shared, and in which users are isolated from diverse viewpoints. These fears are further fuelled by **algorithmic bias**, or **filter bubbles**, whereby social media algorithms personalise content feeds and present users with information that reinforces their attitudes and beliefs (Hartmann et al., 2025; Putri et al., 2024). Moreover, traditional media has also become fragmented into niches of localised interest, including ideological news sources and even ideological talk shows (Arceneaux et al., 2013).

12.3.1 Selective Exposure and Attitude Polarisation

When people can choose which information to read, they use available cues to predict whether it will be consistent with or inconsistent with their attitude. For instance, they may base their choices on what they know about the source, such as the name of the TV channel or its political affiliation. As a result, they engage in **selective exposure** – also known as **biased information search** – whereby they seek out evidence that confirms their existing beliefs. They choose sources that they expect to be sympathetic and non-threatening, and which will confirm rather than disconfirm their point of view. They read arguments from their own groups and avoid those from opposing groups (Taber & Lodge, 2006). For instance, conservatives tend to watch Fox News and avoid CNN and NPR, whereas liberals do the opposite (Iyengar & Hahn, 2009). Furthermore, this effect is more pronounced among those with a relatively high level of political knowledge (Taber & Lodge, 2006) and among the more politically engaged (Iyengar & Hahn, 2009). This has been observed

Echo chambers. Media environments in which only ideas, information, beliefs, and attitudes that align with the user's point of view are shared, and in which users are isolated from diverse viewpoints.

Selective exposure. It involves seeking information that is consistent with one's current attitudes and disregarding or avoiding information that contradicts them.

not only with regard to news about political issues but also "soft" political news, such as crime and travel reports (Iyengar & Hahn, 2009). While strong attitudes generally lead to increased selective exposure, the opposite can sometimes be true. Sawicki et al. (2011) demonstrated that high attitude certainty results in the selection of more attitude-consistent information, but only when this information is familiar to the respondent. However, when the information was relatively unfamiliar, it was the uncertain respondents who were more willing to seek out attitudinally consistent information. Therefore, the **familiarity of the information** may moderate the tendency towards selective exposure.

Ideological polarisation (also attitudinal polarisation). Diverging opinions, beliefs, and attitudes of various groups towards various issues in society.

The tendency for selective exposure is a cause for concern regarding the increasing polarisation of society. There are two types of polarisation: **affective polarisation**, which involves evaluating one's own group positively and treating an outgroup with animosity (see Section 11.4), and **ideological or attitudinal polarisation**, which is characterised by diverging opinions, beliefs, and attitudes towards various issues (Kubin & Sikorski, 2021). Indeed, research confirms that exposure to like-minded sources leads to both types of polarisation (Hartmann et al., 2025). In this context, the question arises as to how this tendency towards selective exposure can be reduced. Some studies have shown that news media literacy campaigns can help achieve this. Relatively short online messages, for example, can inform people about how their personal viewpoints influence their interpretation of the news, while emphasising the importance of being an informed citizen (Vraga & Tully, 2019).

12.3.2 Increasing Openness to Opposing Viewpoints and Depolarisation of Attitudes

Opening up to different viewpoints is beneficial for society and democracy, so finding ways to achieve this is a valuable area of research. **Two-sided messages** (see Section 5.3.2) could be an effective way of encouraging people to be more open to opposing views. They may be particularly effective for individuals with **morally based attitudes** who are otherwise reluctant to consider the other side of an issue. Counterattitudinal two-sided messages – those presenting arguments for and against an issue, while also indicating that the source opposes the recipient's position – increase receivers' openness to counterattitudinal advocacy if they have morally based attitudes. However, this strategy is only effective if the message acknowledges the recipient's point of view respectfully (Xu & Petty, 2022). Furthermore, this effect primarily occurs when the **acknowledgement of the recipient's viewpoint** is placed at the end rather than the beginning of the message. This relates to the perception of the source's thoughtfulness and sincerity (Xu & Petty, 2025).

> **Argumentative ambiguity**. Presenting arguments for and against an issue within a single message, without declaring or suggesting support for either side.

These results suggest that people's tendency to seek out information that supports their point of view, while avoiding exposure to opposing views, may be circumvented by incorporating counterattitudinal information alongside pro-attitudinal information. One approach could be to use **argumentative ambiguity**. This involves presenting both pro- and anti-attitudinal viewpoints on an issue within a single message, without declaring support for either viewpoint (Koniak & Cwalina, 2025). However, Lord et al.'s (1979) studies raised concerns that this approach could result in attitude polarisation (see Section 4.2). Nevertheless, the tendency to polarise attitudes in response to mixed information is not a universal pattern of results. First, the methodology of these studies was specific and actually prompted biased processing of the information presented. Two sources presented contrary arguments: one presented pro-attitudinal information, while the other presented counterattitudinal arguments. Therefore, respondents could agree with one source and disagree with the other. Furthermore, respondents were asked to evaluate each piece of information individually. This facilitated people engaging in biased assimilation, whereby they perceived pro-attitudinal arguments as more persuasive than counterattitudinal ones (see Section 8.2). As a result, receivers' initial attitudes towards a given issue tend to polarise.

However, when pro- and counterattitudinal information comes from the same source and is embedded in an argumentatively ambiguous message, receivers' attitudes **depolarise**, that is, move in the opposite direction to the initial attitude (Koniak & Cwalina, 2022a). Furthermore, ambiguous messages may help to avoid evoking objections from recipients to the information presented. Recipients expressed a comparable level of agreement with argumentatively ambiguous messages as with messages that supported their viewpoint (Koniak & Cwalina, 2022b). Therefore, the way in which information is presented can significantly impact whether receivers' attitudes polarise or depolarise.

Further Reading

Lukianoff, G., & Haidt, J. (2018). *The coddling of the American mind: How good intentions and bad ideas are setting up a generation for failure.* New York: Penguin Books.

12.4 Self-defence against Malevolent Persuasion

The research perspective on attitude change usually focuses on persuading people. In this line of research, resistance is often viewed as an obstacle to be overcome. However, the goal may sometimes be the reverse: ensuring that people will not be persuaded. One example of this is creating strong attitudes to ensure that counter-persuasion will not work (see Chapter 8). In other cases, the goal is not so much to keep the attitudes created as a result of our persuasive attempts unchanged but rather to prepare people to resist various potentially negative messages that may appear on social communication networks. This is particularly important at a time when **fake news, conspiracy theories, misinformation, and propaganda** are rife. All of these can be treated as examples of **malevolent persuasion**: people are being persuaded that vaccines cause autism, that the attack on a sovereign country was provoked, that the moon landing didn't happen, and so on. Studies on misinformation correction show that **debunking false information** is not easy. Therefore, a **proactive strategy of forewarning** people and preparing them for such misleading attempts may be helpful (Lewandowsky & van der Linden, 2021). Similarly, it is better to prepare people to recognise and cope with **deceptive marketing practices** than to alleviate losses afterwards. After all, an ounce of prevention is worth a pound of cure.

12.4.1 Inoculation Theory

William McGuire (1964, 1970) proposed that people could be immunised against attempts to influence their beliefs in the same way that they are immunised against viruses – by taking small dose of the attacking material. This attack should be strong enough to stimulate defensive reaction but not so strong as to overwhelm it. McGuire (1970) called this the **vaccine for brainwash**. Thus, people can be inoculated against potentially harmful ideas, messages, and information (see, e.g., Banas & Rains, 2010; Compton, 2012).

The basic scheme ofinoculation theory research includes presenting attack messages to all participants. However, only some participants receive a **pre-treatment** message before the attack. This allows us to see whether the attack is effective and whether the pre-treatment protected the receivers from its influence. Pre-treatment typically involves presenting a **refutational statement** containing arguments from the attacking side, as well as arguments that refute and weaken their impact. Most studies confirm that participants who received pre-treatment inoculation were more resistant to subsequent attacks than those in the control group. Furthermore, **supportive treatment** – treatment that includes only arguments in support of the receiver's attitude, with no attacking element – is not a very effective form of inoculation. This theory describes it as being like taking vitamins: better than nothing but not as effective as vaccination.

Pre-treatment message. The message presenting before the attacking message.

Refutational statement. Part of pre-treatment message containing arguments from the attacking side, as well as arguments that refuted and weakened their impact.

Supportive treatment. Pre-treatment that includes only arguments in support of the receiver's attitude, with no attacking element.

For inoculation to be effective, the **threat** must appear, as this motivates the recipient to reinforce their pre-attack attitude. The threat may be **implicit**, such as when the presence of a counterattitudinal message threatens an existing attitude. Alternatively, it may be **explicit**, as in the case of a forewarning included in the inoculation message indicating the receiver's attitude is right but may be attacked. A second factor conditioning the effectiveness of inoculation is **refutational pre-emption**, that is, information that the recipient can use to fend off an attack and strengthen their own attitude. This enables the receiver to practise the process of counter-argumentation and defence of their attitude. This may be argumentation used in a subsequent attacking message (**refutational-same**) or argumentation not included in the attacking message (**refutational-different**). The effectiveness of "refutational-same" and "refutational-different" treatments is similar. Therefore, the effectiveness of inoculation treatments does not simply depend on providing recipients with ready-made arguments. The objective of the pre-treatment is to activate the recipient to develop their own counterargumentation in response to the subsequent attack (metaphorically speaking, the goal of the pre-treatment is to create "antibodies").

The effectiveness of the inoculation treatment has been confirmed in various contexts, including health, politics, and marketing (Compton, 2012). Research has also shown that inoculation can help combat the spread of fake news and misinformation (Lewandowsky & van der Linden, 2021) and induce resistance to conspiracy theory propaganda (Banas & Miller, 2013). Furthermore, it has been suggested that inoculation could prevent the adoption of violent extremist ideologies and reduce the intention to support such groups (Braddock, 2019).

Cultural truisms. Beliefs that are accepted without question or challenge.

Fake expert strategy. The use of spokespeople who convey the impression of expertise without possessing any relevant scientific expertise.

The inoculation treatment is effective not only for those whose initial attitudes align with the protected position; it can also create the desired attitude among those who are neutral or opposed. Furthermore, it protects these **newly formed attitudes** from subsequent attacks (Ivanov et al., 2017). The effectiveness of inoculation is not limited to attitudes. Initially, this line of research focused on **cultural truisms**, that is, beliefs that are accepted without question (e.g., "you should brush your teeth daily"). **Values** can also be considered examples of such truisms, as people rarely have the opportunity to develop cognitive support for them, making values an easy target for persuasive attacks (see Section 8.3). However, inoculation pre-treatment can increase the resistance of values to attack. Indeed, an attack on previously inoculated values may even increase their importance to people. Moreover, inoculation against one value can also increase the immunity of other relevant attitudes and values (Bernard et al., 2003). Similarly, Parker et al. (2012) demonstrated that an inoculation focused on attitudes towards unprotected sex reduced the effectiveness of an attack message intended to change not only attitudes towards unprotected sex but also towards other risky behaviours such as binge drinking.

Lewandowsky and van der Linden (2021) discuss various novel perspectives on inoculation and its application. They argue that inoculation can prepare people to recognise and respond to manipulation and persuasion techniques in general. For example, they demonstrate that inoculation can equip individuals to resist the **fake expert strategy**, which is defined as "the use of spokespeople who convey the impression of expertise without possessing any relevant scientific expertise" (Cook et al., 2017, p. 11). This strategy was employed by the tobacco industry decades ago and is now used by climate change deniers, who circulate petitions supposedly signed by thousands of scientists claiming that global warming is a hoax. Providing pre-treatment information indicating that some of the signatures were false (e.g., Charles Darwin and members of the Spice

Girls), or that fewer than 1% of signatories had a background in atmospheric or climate science, has been shown to effectively inoculate recipients against subsequent messages employing this petition as an argument (van der Linden et al., 2017). Cook et al. (2017) found that people exposed to the "fake expert" technique in one context (tobacco industry actions) were inoculated against it in another context (climate change). The inoculation strategy has also been shown to prepare people for **astroturfing**, that is, the posting of large numbers of fake comments on social media by bots masquerading as a grassroots community (Zerback et al., 2020).

Astroturfing. The posting of large numbers of fake comments on social media by bots masquerading as a grassroots community.

12.4.2 *Persuasion Knowledge Model*

The Persuasion Knowledge Model (Friestad & Wright, 1994) posits that individuals possess knowledge regarding persuasion. This knowledge is acquired through personal experience, conversations with others, observation of marketers and other persuasive agents, and what people read and hear about advertising and marketing in the media. Furthermore, this knowledge evolves throughout an individual's lifespan. Culturally supplied folk wisdom about persuasion also changes and varies depending on society and time. According to the model, the person being persuaded (i.e., the target of persuasion) is an active participant in the entire process. The outcome of a persuasion attempt by an agent is shaped by three interacting structures of the target's knowledge: **persuasion knowledge** (knowledge about persuasion tactics, beliefs about the effectiveness and appropriateness of various tactics, beliefs about one's own coping tactics, etc.); **knowledge about the agent's** traits, competencies, and goals; knowledge about the issue, product, candidate, or other object of persuasion. Targets use this knowledge to recognise, analyse, and interpret persuasion attempts, and to select appropriate and effective **coping strategies**. Furthermore, this knowledge directs the target's attention to specific aspects of the situation. Therefore, depending on their knowledge, one target may interpret a given behaviour as a persuasion attempt, while another may interpret it as neutral. They may also use different aspects of the situation to determine whether it constitutes a persuasion attempt. Overall, increasing persuasion knowledge enables targets to recognise, understand, and evaluate persuasion attempts. An increase in persuasion knowledge may be a factor that at least partially explains the reduction in advertising effectiveness. Eisend and Tarrahi (2022) concluded that, while persuasion knowledge cannot eliminate the effects of persuasion entirely, it can reduce them by up to 50%.

This model has primarily been used in consumer and advertising research, as well as in studies examining **scepticism** towards advertising claims and marketing efforts (Eisend & Tarrahi, 2022). These studies have also examined the factors influencing target consumers' application of their persuasion knowledge. For example, Campbell and Kirmani (2000) demonstrated that inferences about persuasive motives and the perception of the persuasive agent (the salesperson in this instance) are dependent on the **accessibility** of these motives and individuals' **cognitive capacities**. When the salesperson's ulterior motives were highly accessible (e.g., when the salesperson made a flattering compliment before the consumer decided to purchase the clothes, or when such motives were primed by an unrelated article that had previously been read), cognitive capacities played no role. In this case, cognitively busy and unbusy people both applied their knowledge of persuasion, resulting in them perceiving the salesperson as less sincere. However, when ulterior motives were less accessible (e.g., the salesperson made a flattering compliment after the consumer had decided to purchase the item, or the ulterior motives were not primed by an unrelated article read previously), cognitively busy people applied their persuasion knowledge to a lesser degree. Consequently, they evaluated the salesperson as more sincere than cognitively unbusy people did.

In the context of self-defence against manipulative messages, it is important to note that people's knowledge of persuasion may not only be activated but also broadened. People can be effectively **taught to recognise and cope with deceptive persuasion attempts**. Boush, Friestad, and Wright (2009) provide a review of deceptive persuasion tactics, as well as examples of studies that have attempted to increase people's knowledge and coping abilities. For instance, Kardes et al. (2006) examined the effectiveness of enhancing individuals' **sensitivity to missing information**. Various types of persuasive messages emphasise information that persuaders want receivers to know and notice, while omitting information that persuaders do not want receivers to know. Such sensitivity can be effectively increased by asking consumers to consider their judgement criteria before product information is presented, or by asking them to rate the presented and missing product attributes before expressing an attitude towards the product.

Further Readings

Boush, D. M., Friestad, M., & Wright, P. (2009). *Deception in the marketplace: The psychology of deceptive persuasion and consumer self-protection*. New York: Routledge.

van der Linden, S. (2023). *Foolproof: Why misinformation infects our minds and how to build immunity*. New York: W. W. Norton & Company.

References

Aaker, J. L., & Lee, A. Y. (2001). "I" seek pleasures and "we" avoid pains: The role of self-regulatory goals in information processing and persuasion. *Journal of Consumer Research, 28*(1), 33–49.

Aaker, J. L., & Maheswaran, D. (1997). The effect of cultural orientation on persuasion. *Journal of Consumer Research, 24*(3), 315–328.

Aaker, J. L., & Williams, P. (1998). Empathy versus pride: The influence of emotional appeals across cultures. *Journal of Consumer Research, 25*(3), 241–261.

Albarracin, D., & Shavitt, S. (2018). Attitudes and attitude change. *Annual Review of Psychology, 69*, 299–327.

Aquino, A., Alparone, F. R., Haddock, G., Maio, G. R., & Wolf, L. J. (2025). Affective-cognitive matching in persuasion: Similarities and differences among three intrapsychic perspectives. In R. E. Petty, A. Luttrell, & J. D. Teeny (Eds.), *The Handbook of personalized persuasion: Theory and application* (pp. 47–70). New York: Routledge.

Arceneaux, K., Johnson, M., & Cryderman, J. (2013). Communication, persuasion, and the conditioning value of selective exposure: Like minds may unite and divide but they mostly tune out. *Political Communication, 30*(2), 213–231.

Avnet, T., Laufer, D., & Higgins, E. T. (2013). Are all experiences of fit created equal? Two paths to persuasion. *Journal of Consumer Psychology, 23*(3), 301–316.

Banas, J. A., & Miller, G. (2013). Inducing resistance to conspiracy theory propaganda: Testing inoculation and metainoculation strategies. *Human Communication Research, 39*(2), 184–207.

Banas, J. A., & Rains, S. A. (2010). A meta-analysis of research on inoculation theory. *Communication Monographs, 77*(3), 281–311.

Bernard, M. M., Maio, G. R., & Olson, J. M. (2003). The vulnerability of values to attack: Inoculation of values and value-relevant attitudes. *Personality & Social Psychology Bulletin, 29*(1), 63–75.

Boush, D. M., Friestad, M., & Wright, P. (2009). *Deception in the marketplace: The psychology of deceptive persuasion and consumer self-protection*. New York: Routledge.

Braddock, K. (2019). Vaccinating against hate: Using attitudinal inoculation to confer resistance to persuasion by extremist propaganda. *Terrorism and Political Violence, 34*(2), 240–262.

Campbell, M. C., & Kirmani, A. (2000). Consumers' use of persuasion knowledge: The effects of accessibility and cognitive capacity on perceptions of an influence agent. *Journal of Consumer Research, 27*(1), 69–83.

Cesario, J., Corker, K. S., & Jelinek, S. (2013). A self-regulatory framework for message framing. *Journal of Experimental Social Psychology, 49*(2), 238–249.

Cesario, J., Grant, H., & Higgins, E. T. (2004). Regulatory fit and persuasion: Transfer from "feeling right.". *Journal of Personality and Social Psychology, 86*(3), 388–404.

Cesario, J., & Higgins, E. T. (2008). Making message recipients "feel right": How nonverbal cues can increase persuasion. *Psychological Science, 19*(5), 415–420.

Cesario, J., Higgins, E. T., & Scholer, A. A. (2008). Regulatory fit and persuasion: Basic principles and remaining questions. *Social and Personality Psychology Compass, 2*(1), 444–463.

Compton, J. (2012). Inoculation theory. In J. P. Dillard, & L. Shen (Eds.), *The Sage handbook of persuasion: Developments in theory and practice* (2nd ed., pp. 220–236). Thousand Oaks, CA: Sage Publications.

Cook, J., Lewandowsky, S., & Ecker, U. K. H. (2017). Neutralizing misinformation through inoculation: Exposing misleading argumentation techniques reduces their influence. *PLOS One, 12*(5), e0175799.

DeBono, K. G., & Harnish, R. J. (1988). Source expertise, source attractiveness, and the processing of persuasive information: A functional approach. *Journal of Personality and Social Psychology, 55*(4), 541–546.

Eisend, M., & Tarrahi, F. (2022). Persuasion knowledge in the marketplace: A meta-analysis. *Journal of Consumer Psychology, 32*(1), 3–22.

Fabrigar, L. R., & Petty, R. E. (1999). The role of the affective and cognitive bases of attitudes in susceptibility to affectively and cognitively based persuasion. *Personality and Social Psychology Bulletin, 25*(3), 363–381.

Friestad, M., & Wright, P. (1994). The persuasion knowledge model: How people cope with persuasion attempts. *Journal of Consumer Research, 21*(1), 1–31.

Han, S. P., & Shavitt, S. (1994). Persuasion and culture: Advertising appeals in individualistic and collectivistic societies. *Journal of Experimental Social Psychology, 30*(4), 326–350.

Hartmann, D., Wang, S. M., Pohlmann, L., & Berendt, B. (2025). A systematic review of echo chamber research: Comparative analysis of conceptualizations, operationalizations, and varying outcomes. *Journal of Computational Social Science, 8*(52).

Higgins, E. T. (1998). Promotion and prevention: Regulatory focus as a motivational principle. In M. P. Zanna (Ed.), *Advances in experimental social psychology: Vol. 30* (pp. 1–46). New York: Academic Press.

Higgins, E. T. (2005). Value from regulatory fit. *Current Directions in Psychological Science, 14*(4), 209–213.

Hong, J., & Chang, H. H. (2015). "I" follow my heart and "we" rely on reasons: The impact of self-construal on reliance on feelings versus reasons in decision making. *Journal of Consumer Research, 41*(6), 1392–1411.

Hornikx, J., & O'Keefe, D. J. (2009). Adapting consumer advertising appeals to cultural values: A meta-analytic review of effects on persuasiveness and ad liking. *Communication Yearbook, 33*(1), 39–71.

Huang, Y., & Shen, F. (2016). Effects of cultural tailoring on persuasion in cancer communication: A meta-analysis. *Journal of Communication, 66*(4), 694–715.

Ivanov, B., Rains, S. A., Geegan, S. A., Vos, S. C., Haarstad, N. D., & Parker, K. A. (2017). Beyond simple inoculation: Examining the persuasive value of inoculation for audiences with initially neutral or opposing attitudes. *Western Journal of Communication, 81*(1), 105–126.

Iyengar, S., & Hahn, K. S. (2009). Red media, blue media: Evidence of ideological selectivity in media use. *Journal of Communication, 59*(1), 19–39.

Joyal-Desmarais, K., Rothman, A. J., & Snyder, M. (2025). Motivational message matching and the functional approach to personalized persuasion. In R. E. Petty, A. Luttrell, & J. D. Teeny (Eds.), *The handbook of personalized persuasion: Theory and application* (pp. 23–46). New York: Routledge.

Joyal-Desmarais, K., Scharmer, A. K., Madzelan, M. K., See, J. V., Rothman, A. J., & Snyder, M. (2022). Appealing to motivation to change attitudes, intentions, and

behavior: A systematic review and meta-analysis of 702 experimental tests of the effects of motivational message matching on persuasion. *Psychological Bulletin, 148*(7–8), 465–517.
Julka, D. L., & Marsh, K. L. (2000). Matching persuasive messages to experimentally induced needs. *Current Research in Social Psychology, 5*(21), 1–19.
Kardes, F. R., Posavac, S. S., Silvera, D., Cronley, M. L., Sanbonmatsu, D. M., Schertzer, S., Miller, F., Herr, P. M., & Chandrashekaran, M. (2006). Debiasing omission neglect. *Journal of Business Research, 59*(6), 786–792.
Koenig, A. M., Cesario, J., Molden, D. C., Kosloff, S., & Higgins, E. T. (2009). Incidental experiences of regulatory fit and the processing of persuasive appeals. *Personality and Social Psychology Bulletin, 35*(10), 1342–1355.
Koniak, P., & Cwalina, W. (2022a). Forbid/allow asymmetry in persuasion: The forbid frame decreases biased elaboration and increases attitude change. *Social Psychology, 53*(1), 1–20.
Koniak, P., & Cwalina, W. (2022b). Does it pay to avoid speaking straight about controversial issues? Impact of argumentative ambiguity on the perception of the speaker. *Journal of Communication Management, 26*(1), 84–97.
Koniak, P., & Cwalina, W. (2025). Ambiguity. In A. Nai, M. Grömping, & D. Wirz (Eds.), *Elgar encyclopedia of political communication*. Vol. 1, pp. 62–66. Cheltenham: Edward Elgar Publishing.
Kosinski, M., Stillwell, D., & Graepel, T. (2013). Private traits and attributes are predictable from digital records of human behavior. *Proceedings of the National Academy of Sciences of the United States of America, 110*(15), 5802–5805.
Kubin, E., & von Sikorski, C. (2021). The role of (social) media in political polarization: A systematic review. *Annals of the International Communication Association, 45*(3), 188–206.
Lavine, H., & Snyder, M. (1996). Cognitive processing and the functional matching effect in persuasion: The mediating role of subjective perceptions of message quality. *Journal of Experimental Social Psychology, 32*(6), 580–604.
LeBoeuf, R. A., & Simmons, J. P. (2010). Branding alters attitude functions and reduces the advantage of function-matching persuasive appeals. *Journal of Marketing Research, 47*(2), 348–360.
Lee, A. Y. (2025). Leveraging the promotion and prevention system: A motivational approach to personalized persuasion. In R. E. Petty, A. Luttrell, & J. D. Teeny (Eds.), *The handbook of personalized persuasion: Theory and application* (pp. 94–115). New York: Routledge.
Lewandowsky, S., & van der Linden, S. (2021). Countering misinformation and fake news through inoculation and prebunking. *European Review of Social Psychology, 32*(2), 348–384.
Lord, C. G., Ross, L., & Lepper, M. R. (1979). Biased assimilation and attitude polarization: The effects of prior theories on subsequently considered evidence. *Journal of Personality and Social Psychology, 37*(11), 2098–2109.
Lukianoff, G., & Haidt, J. (2018). *The coddling of the American mind: How good intentions and bad ideas are setting up a generation for failure*. New York: Penguin Books.
McGuire, W. J. (1964). Inducing resistance to persuasion: Some contemporary approaches. In L. Berkowitz (Ed.), *Advances in experimental social psychology* (Vol. 1, pp. 191–229). New York: Academic Press.

McGuire, W. J. (1970). Vaccine for brainwash. *Psychology Today, 3*(9), 36–64.

Ng, A. H., Hynie, M., & MacDonald, T. K. (2012). Culture moderates the pliability of ambivalent attitudes. *Journal of Cross-Cultural Psychology, 43*(8), 1313–1324.

Ng, W. J. R., See, Y. H. M., & Cheung, M. W.-L. (2025). The influence of affective and cognitive appeals on persuasion outcomes: A cross-cultural meta-analysis. *Journal of Communication, 75*(2), 101–111.

Parker, K. A., Ivanov, B., & Compton, J. (2012). Inoculation's efficacy with young adults' risky behaviors: Can inoculation confer cross-protection over related but untreated issues? *Health Communication, 27*(3), 223–233.

Petty, R. E., Luttrell, A., & Teeny, J. D. (Eds.). (2025). *The handbook of personalized persuasion: Theory and application*. New York: Routledge.

Petty, R. E., & Wegener, D. T. (1998). Matching versus mismatching attitude functions: Implications for scrutiny of persuasive messages. *Personality and Social Psychology Bulletin, 24*(3), 227–240.

Putri, S. D. G., Purnomo, E. P., & Khairunissa, T. (2024). Echo chambers and algorithmic bias: The homogenization of online culture in a smart society. *SHS Web of Conferences, 202,* 05001.

Sawicki, V., Wegener, D. T., Clark, J. K., Fabrigar, L. R., Smith, S. M., & Bengal, S. T. (2011). Seeking confirmation in times of doubt: Selective exposure and the motivational strength of weak attitudes. *Social Psychological and Personality Science, 2*(5), 540–546.

Shavitt, S. (1990). The role of attitude objects in attitude functions. *Journal of Experimental Social Psychology, 26*(2), 124–148.

Shavitt, S. (2025). Culture and personalized persuasion. In R. E. Petty, A. Luttrell, & J. D. Teeny (Eds.), *The handbook of personalized persuasion: Theory and application* (pp. 165–190). New York: Routledge.

Shavitt, S., Johnson, T. P., & Zhang, J. (2011). Horizontal and vertical cultural differences in the content of advertising appeals. *Journal of International Consumer Marketing, 23*(3–4), 297–310.

Snyder, M., & DeBono, K. G. (1985). Appeals to image and claims about quality: Understanding the psychology of advertising. *Journal of Personality and Social Psychology, 49*(3), 586–597.

Snyder, M., & Gangestad, S. (1986). On the nature of self-monitoring: Matters of assessment, matters of validity. *Journal of Personality and Social Psychology, 51*(1), 125–139.

Taber, C. S., & Lodge, M. (2006). Motivated skepticism in the evaluation of political beliefs. *American Journal of Political Science, 50*(3), 755–769.

van der Linden, S. (2023). *Foolproof: Why misinformation infects our minds and how to build immunity*. New York: W. W. Norton & Company.

van der Linden, S., Leiserowitz, A., Rosenthal, S., & Maibach, E. (2017). Inoculating the public against misinformation about climate change. *Global Challenges, 1*(2), 1600008.

Vaughn, L. A., Hesse, S. J., Petkova, Z., & Trudeau, L. (2009). "This story is right on": The impact of regulatory fit on narrative engagement and persuasion. *European Journal of Social Psychology, 39*(3), 447–456.

Vraga, E. K., & Tully, M. (2019). Engaging with the other side: Using news media literacy messages to reduce selective exposure and avoidance. *Journal of Information Technology & Politics, 16*(1), 77–86.

Winterich, K. P., Gangwar, M., & Grewal, R. (2018). When celebrities count: Power distance beliefs and celebrity endorsements. *Journal of Marketing*, *82*(3), 70–86.

Xu, M., & Petty, R. E. (2022). Two-sided messages promote openness for morally based attitudes. *Personality and Social Psychology Bulletin*, *48*(8), 1151–1166.

Xu, M., & Petty, R. E. (2025). Order matters when using two-sided messages to influence morally based attitudes. *Personality and Social Psychology Bulletin*, *51*(8), 1456–1471.

Zerback, T., Töpfl, F., & Knöpfle, M. (2020). The disconcerting potential of online disinformation: Persuasive effects of astroturfing comments and three strategies for inoculation against them. *New Media & Society*, *23*(5), 1080–1098.

Zhang, J., & Yang, X. (2015). Stylistic properties and regulatory fit: Examining the role of self-regulatory focus in the effectiveness of an actor's vs. observer's visual perspective. *Journal of Consumer Psychology*, *25*(3), 449–458.

Index

For Product Safety Concerns and Information please contact our EU representative GPSR@taylorandfrancis.com
Taylor & Francis Verlag GmbH, Kaufingerstraße 24, 80331 München, Germany

www.ingramcontent.com/pod-product-compliance
Lightning Source LLC
LaVergne TN
LVHW010659110826
845149LV00014B/3164
* 9 7 8 1 0 3 2 9 6 3 4 6 4 *